National Agricultural Union

Speeches of the Earl of Winchilsea and Nottingham

Delivered at York, Ipswich, Plymouth, Bedford and Bristol,

1893

National Agricultural Union

Speeches of the Earl of Winchilsea and Nottingham Delivered at York, Ipswich, Plymouth, Bedford and Bristol, 1893

ISBN/EAN: 9783337408756

Printed in Europe, USA, Canada, Australia, Japan

Cover: Foto ©Suzi / pixelio.de

More available books at **www.hansebooks.com**

SPEECHES

OF THE

EARL OF WINCHILSEA AND NOTTINGHAM

Delivered at York, Ipswich, Plymouth, Bedford, and Bristol, 1893.

PUBLISHED AT THE OFFICES OF THE "N. A. U. CABLE,"

30 FLEET STREET LONDON E.C.

SUBJECTS DEALT WITH AT YORK.

———•◦•———

SUBJECTS DEALT WITH AT IPSWICH.

SUBJECTS DEALT WITH AT PLYMOUTH.

SUBJECTS DEALT WITH AT BEDFORD.

SUBJECTS DEALT WITH AT BRISTOL.

A·THREEFOLD·CORD·IS·NOT·QUICKLY·BROKEN

NATIONAL THE AGRICULTURAL UNION

CABLE

EDITED·BY·THE·EARL·OF·WINCHILSEA

THE extraordinary progress made by the **National Agricultural Union** since the Scheme was proposed two months ago, and the number of applications received daily for information about it from all parts of the country, have decided LORD WINCHILSEA to bring out

A WEEKLY NEWSPAPER

Edited by himself, and conducted under his own immediate supervision. The paper will be the OFFICIAL ORGAN of the Movement, and will be entitled

"THE National Agricultural Union Cable"

The First Number will appear shortly.

Correspondents are required in **Every Market Town** in the Country. Those willing to help in this department are requested to send a Post-card to Lord WINCHILSEA with their name and address, and the name of the Market Town for which they will make themselves responsible.

Journalists in Agricultural Districts able to supply any *Special Information*, are also asked to place themselves in communication with Lord WINCHILSEA.

Agents for the Sale of the Paper and for **Advertisements** are required everywhere. These should lose no time in communicating with headquarters.

All Letters to be addressed to—

THE EDITOR
" N. A. U. CABLE" Offices,
30, Fleet Street,
London, E.C.

ONE PENNY PER WEEK.

Annual Subscription, Post Free, **6s. 6d.**

PREFACE.

The following speeches record the progress of a movement which, in its aims and methods, is to some extent unique.

Attempts have often been made to form the various classes engaged in the same industry into different associations more or less hostile to each other, sometimes with good effects, but oftener causing strikes, lock-outs, and loss of trade. But here, for the first time, it is proposed to combine them together, on the ground that their interests are really identical, and to apply this new principle to an industry which has hitherto been regarded as the very type of dis-union.

Yet if the principle advocated be sound—and it is daily making fresh converts—it may well be that in the National Agricultural Union a great, perhaps a final, opportunity is afforded, to landlords of recovering something of the position and influence they have lost; to tenants, of making head against the unfair profits of middlemen; and to labourers, of making their own voices heard, of improving their own position, and of shaking off, like a second Sindbad, their veritable Old Man of the Sea, the professional agitator, who fills the ears of his dupes with delusive promises, and his own pockets with their well-earned pence.

Who doubts the gravity of the crisis, who the vast extent of the power to meet it which resides, if they could only use it, in the 8,000,000 people whose fortunes are bound up with the land? Who would not do something to rescue the goodly vessel which now lies at the mercy of wind and waves, yet seeming but to need a disciplined and united crew to bring her, with all the precious freight she bears, safe into port?

Let us all man the "N. A. U." lifeboat, and put out to the rescue. It may be that with a "long pull, a strong pull, and a pull altogether," and by the help of the "N. A. U. Cable," we shall succeed.

Winchilsea.

Haverholme Priory, Sleaford,

NATIONAL
AGRICULTURAL UNION.

———◆———

SPEECH

OF THE

EARL OF WINCHILSEA & NOTTINGHAM.

Delivered at York, January 5th, 1893.

THE EARL OF WINCHILSEA AND NOTTINGHAM : Lord Herries, my Lords, Ladies and Gentlemen, it is a very great honour which you have paid me to-day, and involves on my part a corresponding responsibility. I was told by a shrewd observer two or three days ago that my scheme was all right in itself, and he only questioned whether there was enough common sense in the country to carry it through. (Laughter.) Well, ladies and gentlemen, when we want to find shrewdness and common sense—I do not know why it is so—we always turn instinctively to those parts of England where the breeding of good horses has occupied the population for many generations. I do not in the least defend that proposition or explain it : I simply state it as a well-known fact ; and therefore, in search of common sense on this question, I come naturally to Yorkshire, and to the great capital of your county. (Cheers.)

Now it is not, I think, a very curious thing, but it is a thing which is quite natural, considering that the only opportunities that I have had of explaining this scheme by word of mouth (a plan which I always infinitely, and we all, I think, prefer) have been confined to about five minutes on three occasions at the Agricultural Conference, that the scheme in all its bearings has not yet been sufficiently understood. But I am very glad to notice, by the remarks which have been made by your Chairman, that here at least, in Yorkshire, the "hang" of it, as we say, has really been taken up and understood. I shall not confine myself, of course, though I shall address myself closely, to those questions which your Chairman has indicated to me as those in which you probably, as a conference, will take the greatest interest ; but I shall ask you to indulge me patiently while I also place before you the general aspect of the question. Now, ladies and gentlemen, where do we stand at the present moment ? We stand in a position which, twenty years ago, we little thought to have occupied ; and although, as I have said, I feel a difficulty in addressing you corresponding with the responsibility which rests upon me, still I do say that after you and I, as fellow-agriculturists, have passed through the experiences of the last fifteen or twenty years, a man may speak to you from his heart as I do to-day ; and I think that you will say to any individual, however humble, " If you have a word of counsel at the present crisis, say on."

The Crisis.

Now, where do we stand ? We stand in this position. The great industry by which we live is reduced, if not to ruin—which Lord Herries, with English pluck, is determined not to admit—yet at the' same time to such dire straits that the profits of all the three classes connected with it—the landlord, the labourer, and the tenant—have been reduced almost to a vanishing point ; to such a point that, if things are to be carried further in that direction, I know not whether we may not soon be face to face with bankruptcy. And the curious part of it is, that we are starving in the midst of plenty. The position is unparalleled in the history of the world. We are like that noble of old who stood in the gate of Samaria, and could see the plenty with his eyes, but was not allowed to partake thereof. And even further we are like him, because we are in danger of being trampled to death by the press of our fellow-citizens who are eager to get at this plenty from without. At the very least, we are not a moment too early in addressing ourselves—each of these three classes—to the problem before us, and asking ourselves, " Can we—not by remaining at home and taking no interest in these affairs, but by coming together, class with class, and man with man —do anything to avert the crisis which is possibly impending over what is your greatest national industry in this country ? "

I think that the Agricultural Conference was right in one thing. It decreed—and nobody can deny that it is so—that the present state of things has been brought about very much owing to the fall of prices, which has been the result of foreign competition. (Loud cheers.) When we were masters of the market, when the sea, which has now become, agriculturally, our greatest foe because it brings us everything, it seems to me, for nothing, was still our friend by keeping out the over-production of foreign countries, we were tolerably safe in maintaining an unorganised position. The landlord, as long as he obtained his rent and saw a contented tenantry and a contented peasantry in possession of his estate, had little reason to organise. The tenant, who, as I say, had at that time command of the market, had nothing to do but to go there on his own account, and he could get a good price for that which he brought there. The labourer, at that time at any rate, was secure of wages, because the land was making a good profit, and he occupied himself very little with questions outside his daily career.

Competition and Disorganisation.

But I submit to you that the very moment that you get competition in the aggravated form in which it now exists, the conditions are entirely altered, for what has competition enabled the middleman to do ? He, being organised, and you not, it has put a weapon into his hands which has enabled him to do this—and certainly it was a very happy thought which dictated to him the idea on his own account—it has enabled him to give you as producers only the price which foreign things command, and still to charge the consumer the same high price which English things used to obtain. This is a point which I wish to draw your special attention to as men of business. If the consumer at this moment were only paying a trifle more for what he eats and consumes than you are getting for what you produce, I should say that organisation, from that point of view only, would do you little good, because I do not think that you will ever be able entirely to do away with the middleman as a distributor. His fair profits are best left in his hands. But I ask you, Is that so, or is it not? Is there not an enormous profit now being divided, sufficient in many cases—notably in the case of rearing stock—to make the difference between profit and loss, in the industry in which we are engaged? Now, if that be so, I shall hope, when I address myself to that portion of my remarks which will deal with co-operation, to show you that the profit of the middleman—not the legitimate profit, but what I shall show you is very nearly a fraudulent profit—may be shared between you and the consumer by co-operation to the mutual advantage of both.

Railway Rates.

Now what is another result of this disorganisation of the agricultural interest? Why, that every interest which does not wish to pay its fair share of the rates and taxes of this country, and is sufficiently organised to get the public ear, has placed those burdens on you and me. And, secondly, there is that most important point to which Lord Herries, in his opening remarks, addressed himself—that the railway companies have dealt with you and me as they never would have dared to do with an organised interest as great as your own. (Cheers).

Upon this particular point I will read you a letter which appeared in the *Standard* of the 2nd January, and I would commend it to the earnest attention of agriculturists all over the kingdom. The letter is signed by Mr. Clarke, and it says this:—" The increase in railway rates is nothing less than a deathblow to a large section of the farming interest. For some years past many enterprising farmers have turned their attention to growing carrots, parsnips, brocoli, onions, peas, &c., for London and other large towns; but the new rates will inevitably put an end to all attempts in that direction." He gives those new rates, and I must say that, prepared as I was for much that was almost incredible, I was surprised by what follows. He says that the increased rates—not the rates, but the increased rates — upon carrots, onions, cabbage, brocoli, and beetroot, vary from £3 1s. per acre in the case of carrots, up to £14 11s. 3d. an acre in the case of beetroot. That is the increased rate which the railway companies dare to charge you for sending that produce to London. And he pertinently asks, " What are rates and taxes, what is rent, compared with such monstrous impositions as this?" And he says, " If any minister had proposed such a tax he would have been howled out of office amid the execrations of his countrymen." Yes, and I go a little further, and I say that when we are properly organised he will be turned out of office if he allows it.

Now, gentlemen, I have shown you so far, I think, from statistics which I have quoted, that, however bad for you competition may have been, disorganisation in addition to it has almost completed your ruin; and I have given you as instances the profits which it has enabled the middleman to make, the rates which have been placed unfairly upon landed property, and the increased rates which railway companies, even when they know what the depression is, and even since the agricultural conference, have allowed themselves cruelly to place upon the interest to which you belong. (Cheers.)

The True Remedy.

What, then, is the obvious, what is the very first condition which we have to fulfil if we would meet these difficulties? Competition in one form or another will be always with us. Whatever you do you cannot hope to eliminate that. But I say that upon the other heading we may do much; we may do everything. We must organise; we must unite; we must present a bold front. We must show that the interests of all classes connected with the land in this matter are one and the same; and we must take such steps as will convince the country that we are now at last, and perhaps for the first time, in earnest, and that we mean what we say. (Cheers.)

The Scheme.

Well, gentlemen, what is the scheme? For my object in accepting your invitation to come here to-day is not merely to give you these general truths, with which you probably are as well acquainted as I am, but to give you a specific, which I hope may act as a palliative, and eventually, perhaps, as a remedy for the evils to which I have referred. I want to place before you what I believe to be a plain business-like scheme, by which we shall be able to unite for the defence of our common interests.

Now, in case there may be present any gentlemen who are not familiar with the details of that scheme, I shall not venture to trust to my memory, because, of course, I am addressing many outside these walls, but if your patience will allow me I shall read to you exactly what it is that I propose. I propose that the name of the society shall be the National Agricultural Union; that its objects shall be—"To frame such measures as may from time to time be needful in the agricultural interest; to organise in every constituency a body of public opinion favourable to the return, without distinction of party, of candidates who support the programme of the Union "—(cheers)—" and generally to promote the co-operation of all persons connected with the land, whether as owners, occupiers, or labourers, for the common good. Membership shall be open to all persons of whatever class who are interested in the land of the United Kingdom." The annual subscriptions payable by members I have fixed upon a basis which, of course, finds a place in the draft scheme; but this point in connection with it I do rather press upon the attention of this meeting. I have made a sliding scale by which owners will be asked to contribute in proportion to the number of acres which we, as a Union, shall assist in protecting from spoilation. I do not think that is unfair, because the part which each class will take in making this Union a success must be rather a different one. They will all belong to it; but I make no secret of the fact that we cannot carry on this Union without money.

That, I think, will commend itself to a Yorkshire audience as a not too extravagant statement; and for that money we shall have to draw upon the landlords. If this thing is not to be a plaything; but if we are really to make it into a serviceable tool, we must not play with it, but we must give according to our ability. If we do not believe that it is of any use to us, pass it on one side, and occupy neither your time nor mine any longer with it. But if we take it up, I do ask you to do as I have done in one particular: devote a good part of your time—at any rate until it is made a success—to making other people understand it as thoroughly as, I hope, before the end of this meeting, you will understand it yourselves. And I do say this to landlords, if I may. Many of them by their presence here to-day have indicated that they can give a considerable portion of their time to the work of the Union; but if they cannot give their time, yet there is one very simple thing which it will only take them two minutes to do ; first of all, to calculate what their subscription will be according to the acreage of their estate, and then to give a standing order to their bankers to pay it from year to year. (Cheers and laughter.)

I propose that the central offices of the Union shall be in London, and that the whole control and management of its affairs shall be vested in a council consisting of elected delegates. This is a point to which I hope to recur rather later in my remarks; but let me lay it down as a proposition here and now, which I think I can prove the truth of, that if we are to make this Union a success we must get all three classes to join it; and I am now thinking particularly of the labourers, and they will not join it unless they are assured of fair and equal representation upon the control of it.

Progress already Made.

Now, gentlemen, let me ask you for one minute to follow me while I indicate to you what has been the progress which this scheme has made in public opinion during the short time which has elapsed—only four weeks— since the Agricultural Conference was held. Let me express my great acknowledgments—and I think that in future times, perhaps, the agricultural interest will join me in the expression—to the gentlemen of the press throughout this country for the way in which they have taken up this question. I have nothing whatever to complain of in the criticisms which have been addressed to me by the public press. They have taken me at my word, and it is the greatest compliment which they could have paid me. They may think that I am wrong in certain things which I propose, but they credit me, I am thankful to say, with an honest effort to do that which I say I want to do, which is to combine the agricultural interest simply for the defence of that which we all have an interest in in common. Cheers.)

"Casting its Shadow Before."

But there is a still more significant fact. What was the first feeling manifested in the public press after the Conference in London ? Disappointment. Nobody could read the papers without seeing that. They hoped that we should have proposed something which the country would have been able to accept. From that first feeling, when it passed away, there developed, as it were, a tiny spark of light. They saw something practical in the proposal which I had the honour to introduce, and from that moment the attitude of the press to the demands of agriculture has changed to one not only of sympathy, but also of respect. They see and believe that we mean to organise ourselves, and that we shall be a factor to be taken into account in the public life of this country ; and I say, gentlemen, that that is a fact which you may well take note of, for what is it but the National Agricultural Union casting its shadow before ? That is what it is. (Cheers.) If the public press, representing the country, esteems you and respects you the very moment that you threaten to organise, what will it do when you are organised as you ought to be, and as you will be within six months of the present time ? (Cheers.)

Conditions of Success.

Now, ladies and gentlemen, let us for one moment consider the conditions under which alone such a Union as I propose can be successful.

First of all, it assumes that the interests of the three classes proposed to be combined are one and the same. I have been very much struck with the fact that, although the details of the scheme have been assailed, that central proposition has never once been assailed even by the Radical press, and therefore we may suppose that it is unassailable. But I am told it is a truism to say that our interests are the same. Gentlemen, I hold that a grievance is always a grievance until it has been redressed, and that a truth can never be said to be a truism until it is acted upon; and I ask you, are we, the agricultural interest, at the present moment so organised or so acting as to lead people to believe—nay, do we entirely believe ourselves in our heart of hearts—that there is no difference at all between the interests of the three classes? On the contrary, we are maintaining at the present moment far too much isolation between the three, and the danger is, that if we do so we shall not stop here, but that organisations will be formed—nay, they are now being formed in different parts of the country—not between all the three classes, but separately for each class; and from that there is a very small step to their being organised in a spirit of hostility the one to the other. (Cheers.)

We stand at a point from which we must either advance or retire. The country has taken up this question of an Agricultural Union and placed it now, I think, beyond the possibility of doubt that in one shape or another it will be organised. It rests, gentlemen, with you to say whether you will take that part in it to which interest and duty alike call you; because, if you will not, you cannot complain if the agricultural labourers, for instance, seeing that you will not organise with them, and therefore that you believe that their interests are not the same as yours, organise on their own account. Nor can you afterwards have much ground of complaint if you find that they will not be led or ruled by your counsels, and they may even go in an opposite direction to that in which your interests would lead them to go. (Cheers.)

The Rock on which we Build.

Gentlemen, I have said that we must start, as it were, upon a rock. We must build ourselves upon a solid foundation which cannot be assailed. That foundation I hold to be, that the interests of all three classes are identical. Shall we examine that for one moment and see?

Our Interests are Identical.

At the present moment, what is the interest of a landlord in this country? What does he want better or more than to have a tenantry upon his estate who have sufficient capital and sufficient enterprise to carry on their business at a profit? What does he want more than to have a happy, contented peasantry who are ready to assist the tenantry in the manual labour of the cultivation of the soil? On the other hand, the tenant requires to have the labourers upon the soil, or he cannot carry out his business. It is to his interest and advantage—and may I impress this very deeply upon those who have not studied that point—to get good men upon the land, and to prevent them, if possible, from going into the towns. (Cheers.) And what is the interest of the labourers? This is a point which, in order that I may not take up too much of the time of this meeting, I shall deal with more fully at Ipswich at a meeting at which I have been invited to address the labourers especially; but at the present moment, at any rate, I cannot say less than this, that the interests of the labourers lie, and I believe always will lie, principally in the direction of permanent and regular employment and good wages. (Cheers.) But, of course, there are other inducements which he can be and may be offered, such as a share in the soil to till it in his spare time, and anything which will enable him to turn that spare time, which really is a labourer's spare capital, to the very best account. To sum it up in one word, the interest of all three classes is to make the land produce as much as it can, and to sell the produce for as good a price as they can get for it, so that each one's share of the profits may be as large as possible.

Division of Profits.

Of course, there may be a point at which those interests diverge. You may say, "How shall we agree as to the division of those profits?" Well, gentlemen, we are spared all trouble upon that point at the present moment by the fact that the profits themselves have disappeared altogether. (Laughter.) Our objects now are to get back the profits to the land, and there is no doubt whatever that in that respect our interests are absolutely and entirely one.

I think that we have established that central proposition which is the rock upon which I take my stand—that the interests of all the three classes which it is proposed to combine are identically the same.

The Labourers must be with us.

Now, gentlemen, there is one point which I want to make entirely clear to you at this juncture. I referred to it before, but I refer to it again, because I consider it a cardinal one. You cannot advance a single step for the benefit of the agricultural interest unless you get the labourers, heart and soul and body, with you. (Cheers.) Let me put it to you, if I may, in this way. If a man employs two or three clerks he may be very wise in keeping his business to himself, and merely using them as the instruments for carrying it out. But if he admits his three clerks into partnership with himself, and gives them equal rights of voting with himself, surely then it is the very height of folly to keep what he does from those new partners in his business. Since the last Reform Act the labourers have been partners with you. They have equal votes with you. Their vote counts for as much as my vote or your vote; and therefore I do say that now at any rate it will be wisdom if you treat them no longer as only hired to carry out your commands, but as what they really and essentially are—equal partners with you in your business of extracting food from the soil.

A Tenant Farmers' Union no Use.

It is from this point of view that I am obliged to criticise certain schemes which have made their appearance either before or after the Conference for separate unions of different interests connected with agriculture. I hear, for instance, of a tenant farmers' union. It has a beautiful programme, I believe, among the items of which I find that it is to have a compact body of members to represent it in the House of Commons. But I ask this pertinent question of you—Who is going to return them? Is there a constituency in the United Kingdom in which the tenant farmers at this moment, without the assistance of their labourers, can return a single member? I believe there is a tenant farmer member at the present moment in the House of Commons. As he is not personally known to me it would be too familiar on my part if I were to call him "a party;" and certainly, if I were to call him a solid or compact party, I should be erring still further in that direction. But, gentlemen, I must say that I think that the tenant farmers of this country are not consulting their true interests when they attempt to set up—or if they do so—a union from which the landowners and labourers are specifically excluded; because if they do, how can they expect the labourers, for instance, to take it in any other light than this: "You are offered a union in which we may join, and you will not join, but prefer one of your own. Your interests, therefore, in your own opinion, are different from ours; and can you ask us, therefore, to return as our representative the same man that you would have to represent you?" That will be the question which they will very pertinently ask, and not only will they ask it, but they will answer it. (Cheers.)

It is because I believe that the backbone of this movement ought to be the tenant farmers of this country, inasmuch as they as a class come midway between the landowners and the labourers, that I think that we should look to their personal efforts as much as to the money of the landlords for carrying this scheme right down into our villages, and—let me say it—into the hearts of the agricultural labourers of England; that, therefore, I do in a very friendly spirit, but at the same time with words of respectful warning, ask them not to isolate themselves from the other interests at this great juncture in agriculture, but to come in with us and combine; for I am perfectly certain that, unless we combine, there will be only one thing certain with regard to anything which we ask for, and that is that we shall not get it.

Lord Winchilsea's "Three F's."

Now, of course, when the Union is formed it will be open to any labourer, or any landowner, or any tenant farmer who pleases to bring forward any proposition that he likes before the Union. Take, for instance, "the three F's." Well, I have them on my own estate. I have been farming about 1500 acres of my own land for the last ten years, and, therefore, I have fixity of tenure, because I cannot let it. (Laughter and cheers.) I have free sale, because it belongs to me, and I can do what I like with it. And I have fair rents, because I need not pay any rent at all unless I like. (Laughter.) And yet, gentlemen, oddly enough, I am not entirely contented. I want to disturb that fixity of tenure by letting my land to a tenant. I would forego my privilege of free sale by letting him have a great many of my improvements for nothing. And, with regard to fair rent, I am quite willing to take the same rent from him that I am now making from the land myself. And, let me say in passing that I do make—and I am glad to say that I do make—a rent from my own land which I farm as great as any rent that I ask from my tenants, because I think that is as it should be.

A Fair Landlord.

There are three F's which I should like to see on every estate in this country. I should like to see a fair landlord; I should like to see a free tenant; and I should like to see fixity of labour. When I talk of a fair landlord I mean a man who will do what Lord Herries is doing to-day—interest himself in the great problems of the day (cheers), and show that he thinks it worth while to take some share of personal trouble, even if it is a little inconvenient; to come some distance, even on rather a cold day, to see what can be done for the great interest by which he lives. And by a fair landlord I mean, too, a man who will meet his tenants individually, if they like to come to him, and not deal with them through an agent. (Loud and continued cheers.) Why, good heavens, gentlemen, I speak feelingly, because I know that it can be done. I have three estates in different parts of England, and I have managed them for years without any other agent at all than my principal tenant in each place. (Renewed cheers.)

Free Tenants.

And by free tenants I mean men who have liberty to apply their brains and their capital in the way that seems best to them, within certain common-sense restrictions of course, to the cultivation of the soil.

Fixity of Labour.

And, by fixity of labour I mean a labouring population which no longer wanders from place to place in search of employment, ending too often in our great towns—yes, and finding none. I mean a labouring population which has ties to its home; and a labourer values his home as much as you or I value ours. (Cheers.) I mean a people to whom we can make it worth while, by attaching them to the soil, and letting them get a little profit out of it as we do, to remain in the place where they were born, and to give us the invaluable service of their thews and their sinews in extracting what we want from the land on which we live. (Cheers.) We love the land, and so do they. If you will give me those three F's I fear nothing. I should then have formed such a National Agricultural Union as I hope to form in the future, but as I should then be perfectly certain existed in the present.

Programme of the Union.

Now, ladies and gentlemen, I have been asked, What is the Union to do, and what do I mean by it? Well, Prince Bismarck was said to be the greatest and most successful diplomatist in Europe for one reason, that he always said what he meant and told the truth. People who were engaged in negotiating with him always thought that he must be meaning something different. They were always deceived and always mistaken, and at the end of the time he was able to say, "Very well, I have nothing to re-call; I have nothing to unsay; and if you did not choose to believe what I told you, it was your own fault." In my humble way I occupy something of that sort of position with regard to my critics upon this scheme. I have put forward a perfectly simple idea, but people insist upon crediting me with all sorts of adjuncts and accretions which are not at all in my own mind. I take up my pile of letters in the morning—and I can assure you, gentle-men, that it is not an inconsiderable one at the present moment, because I am enlightened from many directions by people who have "given years of study to this question." I open the first letter and I am encouraged to read, "Dear Lord Winchilsea, I am very glad to join your scheme. I think it is a very good one, and in time, perhaps, I shall subscribe to it. P.S.—Of course you go in for Protection." (Laughter). The next letter, perhaps, I get is from a gentleman who says much the same thing, but his postscript is rather different :—" What 'missing word' nonsense they talked at the Agricultural Conference about Protection." (Laughter). Well, another letter I get politely informs me that the whole thing is a Tory dodge. I open a fourth letter, and I am surprised to find that my careful correspondent cannot see his way to joining it because he is quite certain that it will eventually be captured by the Radicals. (Laughter). And so with other points; but one thing I will say, and that is that the most sensible and the most straight-forward letters which I have received on this subject have been from labourers themselves, simply because they have taken me at my word. They have read my letter to them, and they believe that I honestly desire to do them good. I have a letter from Walsall from a labourer there who said to me, "I and many of my mates like your scheme. I am at work till five o'clock every afternoon, but I mean to devote my evenings to making it known among my own people." Now, I say that I consider it ample reward for any trouble that I may have taken in the matter already, to have deserved, and to have received, the confidence of plain men who read what I say, and do me the compliment to believe that I mean it.

What it is not.

Now, ladies and gentlemen, I of course admit that the Union must have a programme of some sort, and upon the question of what that programme is to be in the immediate future I ask your careful attention for a few minutes, because it is extremely important that it should not be misunderstood. This is to be a Union which I ask all agriculturists to join, on the basis of their common interests, and because they are agriculturists. It is perfectly evident, then, that I have no right to place at the outset, upon the programme of the Union, any point upon which I know that agriculturists are divided. Were I to do so, I should be acting neither honestly nor fairly, and I should defeat my own object, because people of the opposite opinion would not join the Union. What I have done, therefore, I do not think that I can put more plainly than Lord Herries put it in his opening remarks, when he said that it is not for me to lay down, on those disputed points, what the programme of the Union in the future will be; it is for the Union itself, by means of the votes of its members constitutionally given, to decide which of those points upon which we now differ shall be in its programme.

What it is.

But, fortunately, there are subjects upon which we are unanimous. What I desire to do, if you will bear with me for a few minutes longer, is to point out how we propose to deal with the subjects upon which we are unanimous, and also, shortly, how we ought to approach the subjects on which we differ, remembering always that the cardinal principle is union for our common interests, to forward objects on which we are all agreed, and to diminish by discussion among our members the points on which we differ. (Cheers.) Therefore, I thought that I could not do better than sum up the points on which we agree by committing the Union to start with, only to the unanimous resolutions of the Agricultural Conference, because I thought—and I have been supported in that feeling afterwards by many others—that if the Conference was unanimous, elected as it was to represent all the great districts, and even the small districts of this country, we could not be far wrong in supposing that the agricultural interest which it represented was unanimous upon the same points. Therefore, I have ventured to place upon the programme of the Union, to start with, three resolutions upon which the Conference was unanimous; and I think that you will agree with me that, fortunately—I do not say accidentally—they were extremely useful and valuable resolutions.

Its Items.

The first resolution pledges us to obtain a remission of unfair local burdens which now press upon the land. The second is the further protection of our flocks and herds from the ravages of disease—(cheers)—and here we shall get, I believe, great support from the agriculturists of the North of England, for they appear, particularly in Lancashire, to be very warm upon this question. As this is not a contentious subject, and I shall probably not recur to it, I may say in passing that this subject is now under the consideration of a Royal Commission ; and from the deep respect with which we, at the present moment, regard all Royal Commissions—(laughter)—I am quite certain that we may leave it to them. The third, and a very important point too, is that to which I alluded in my opening remarks, namely, the establishment of a system of co-operation between the producers and the consumers, in order to save the inordinate profit of the middleman, to the mutual interest and advantage of both the producer and the consumer. Those are the three points to which the Union is committed from its very start. I think therefore that if you desire, as I believe you do, to form the Union, you probably may desire to hear from me one or two of my views on the practical value of that programme as a present one, and the manner in which those subjects will be approached as soon as we have our organisation together.

Local Taxation—Land Tax.

First of all, upon the question of local taxation, the simple facts are, that the income of this country is about nine hundred millions of money, and it is constantly increasing ; the income from land and houses is about one hundred and sixty millions, and it is constantly decreasing. We, as you see, are responsible for receiving nominally one-sixth of the whole income of the country. Yet, gentlemen, upon that one-sixth falls, almost entirely, the whole of the local burdens of the country. But the case is stronger yet, because it was not always so. Take, for instance, the case of the land tax. Many people may say to me, " Land means land, and, therefore, the land tax must always have been a tax levied upon land." But not at all. The land tax dates from the year 1692, and it was then imposed upon all property, of all kinds, and upon all incomes. In 1798, when Mr. Pitt fixed the land tax at 4s. in the pound, again it was fixed upon all kinds of property ; and it was not, I believe, until 1833 that personal property escaped from taxation to the land tax altogether, for the simple reason that it was found more easy to collect it from us than to collect it from personal property. (Cheers.) There you have, you see again, disorganisation. That is what did it. The land tax collector comes. The man looks at the claim ; he grumbles a bit ; but he pays it, and he goes off and thinks no more about it.

Poor Rate.

In this way the agricultural interest has treated all these local burdens. It has made a broad shoulder, and it has placed that shoulder at the disposal of everybody who chose to place anything upon it, and then we wonder that we are so heavily loaded. (Cheers.) But perhaps I may surprise you when I tell you that it is the same thing with the poor-rate. Whenever we see a poor-rate collector we instinctively put our hands into our pocket, and we instinctively expect the owners of personal property to stand in an attitude which indicates that they have nothing to do with it ; but the poor-rate, equally with the land tax, was seen with great justice, in the days when it was first imposed, in 1601, to be a national concern. It was placed upon the national income, and there again it was not until well on in the present century that land and houses had to bear the full burden of it, and for the very same slipshod reason, perfectly unconnected with justice of any kind, that the collectors, or the Chancellor of the Exchequer, were too lazy to collect it from personal property ; and therefore they put the whole thing upon the broad shoulders of the agricultural interest. (Cheers.) Well, we must point out the justice of being relieved from this burden, and, possibly, from other rates.

Education Rate.

And, while I am talking of other rates, let me say a word about the education rate. Education, too, I think, is, if anything, a national object. If it is not so, why did we pay millions a year out of the National Exchequer towards the education of the poorer children? And, if it is a national object, why does not the nation take it upon its income instead of calling upon you and me to find the balance? It is perfectly right that children in this country should be educated? It is a national duty to see that they are; but I think that it is rather hard that the farmers should be called upon to pay for this, because the first thing that education does is to deprive them of the cheapest form of labour in their fields; and the next thing it does, later on, is to take away all the most intelligent of their labourers into the towns. With regard to the highway rate, we now have, I suppose, a sort of uneasy pricking of the national conscience, in consequence of which we get a considerable Imperial contribution to that rate; but if you and I go to Parliament and urge these matters, as they frequently have been urged, though never quite so strongly as I should like to see them, we are told: "Oh, the whole thing is so complicated, you have no idea what it would involve. I know a Chancellor of the Exchequer who sat for three months doing nothing but thinking how to do it, and he was obliged to give it up." Well, he ought to have given up his office at the same moment. (Cheers.) Gentlemen, the matter is not complicated at all. It is perfectly simple. The complications are in the assessments, which have grown up all over this country, and which not one person in a hundred who pays them can ever understand. That is where the complication is.

Nationalisation of Rates.

It is not for me, of course, to suggest exactly how the remedies can be applied so as to change these burdens from our shoulders to those of the nation; but yet I will offer one or two suggestions which, in default of better ones, may serve to employ my right honourable relative, the Chancellor of the Exchequer, who, doubtless, at this moment has leisure enough to consider them by his own fireside. I must say that I myself have always thought that there is no tax so fair upon everybody, and upon every class of the community, as an income tax, if it is a real one. I do not object to pay the taxes of my country upon my income, after making such deductions as are fair for the upkeep of my land, or my house, or buildings, or whatever it may be. You cannot, I think, impose a fairer tax upon people than to ask them to contribute to the country which protects their interests, on the basis of their income. There is another advantage in the taxation of personal property by this method, which is, that you and I would pay our fair share of it. Landowners and tenants alike pay their fair share, and very often more than their fair share, of the income tax. We should continue to do so still; so that nobody could charge us with having insisted on removing burdens from our own shoulders, and throwing them on to the shoulders of the community at large. We should be bearing our right proportion of them then, just as we are bearing our wrong proportion of them now.

Local Economy and Efficiency Secured.

But then I am told that the difficulty would be, that the local authorities who must spend the money would not care a farthing how much they spent if they could draw on the Imperial Exchequer. Well, I will submit to you, respectfully, a way in which that difficulty might be entirely overcome. Let the Imperial Government do exactly as it does in the matter of the education rate. Let it send down, on the report of efficiency previously received from a Government Inspector, a sum to each local authority as great as, according to the statistics of the country, ought to maintain the poor, to pay the oducation rate, or the highway rate, or whatever it was in that particular locality. Let the local authority remain with its rating powers exactly as at present, and let it spend the Imperial money which is so sent down to it; and if the local authority cannot make the money do, let them lay a rate for the balance. You would find that that would be an admirable, self-acting system. (Cheers.) You would get the maximum of local economy, and also the maximum of Imperial efficiency; for what would happen? Supposing that the local authority, we will say, in York, could make the Imperial contribution do, and did not have to lay a rate, and supposing that the local authority at Thirsk could not make it do, and had to lay a rate, what would the ratepayers say? " Who are these people who cannot conduct our affairs as economically as they can at York? We will change them, and we will have a lot of people (guardians or what not) who can do it;" and you then would have the burden on the proper shoulders, and you would have a thoroughly efficient system, I believe, which would work both economically and fairly to all interests concerned. But, as I have said, it is not really my business to suggest how these things can be done; still, I may say that I think with the Roman poet, "If you can find a better way, by all means let us have it. If not, use mine."

I think with regard to local taxation that if some scheme of that kind could be adopted we should at any rate remove an unjust and very large burden from our own shoulders, and we should carry that which has often been attempted and has hitherto been attempted in vain. But let me go back to my text, and assure you that unless and until you are fully organised, just though your requests may be, unanswerable as your arguments may be found to be, you will still find that those who ought to pay will not be convinced by them, and will continue to turn a deaf ear to you until you bring a little gentle pressure to bear upon them to induce them to listen. (Cheers.)

Now, ladies and gentlemen, it appears to me, therefore, that this is an eminently practical part of our programme, one which, as I have shown to you, can be solved in one very simple way if it cannot be solved in another, and it is one which it is well worth our while to pursue; and if, either in the next or the succeeding session of Parliament, we were only to get local taxation altered and placed on the right shoulders, we should have done a very good stroke of business, which would well justify our having formed a National Agricultural Union. (Cheers.)

Co-operation.

I have said that the question of disease is one which we must leave to that august tribunal which is now engaged in deliberating upon it. I pass to the third question which we have placed upon our programme, the very important one of co-operation. I would draw your attention to this fact for a moment, that all co-operative societies, so far as I know, or the large ones at least, such as the Army and Navy Stores in London, and others with which we are familiar, exist in the sole interests of the consumer, and they are against the producer. Why is that? Because they are enormous buyers. They go into every market, and beat down the price of all the things that they buy, and therefore they are against the producers, and entirely in favour of the consumers. But I think that it is about time in this country that the producer should get a little share of national attention. After all, he is the honey bee, and not the drone. The producer is the man in the nation who creates the national wealth, and we, as producers, have a right, I think, to ask that we shall receive some share of the national sympathy, and we have also a perfect right to combine together for the defence of our interests. I have mentioned this fact to you, but I recur to it again, that at the present moment the profits of the middleman, owing to your not being organised, are so great as in many instances to make the difference between profit and loss to the grower if you could get hold of them.

The Middleman.

Now, take the case of bread, for instance. We have bread in many of our towns at the present moment at very much the same price that it was when wheat was forty shillings a quarter. (Loud cheers.) We have no means of knowing what profit the bakers make, though we very seldom see their names in the Bankruptcy Court. But we have a means of knowing from the official report what a great bread company makes. It was not very many days ago that the chairman of the Aërated Bread Company made a statement to his shareholders which I need not tell you was rapturously received—that owing to their having been able to buy wheat so cheaply, and owing to their having been able to induce the consumers to give something like the old price for bread, he was glad to be able to announce to them a dividend of 30 per cent. upon their capital. Gentlemen, I should like to get hold of a little of that 30 per cent. (Cheers.) And not only was that so, but he distributed among them, as if it was nothing, a little bonus of 7½ per cent. besides, just to take home for pocket money. Well, that is the condition in which the bread trade is. Now let us turn to the meat trade. That is also in a condition which makes agriculturists wild when they think of it. The consumer is paying, at any rate in our large towns, very much the same price that he always paid. At the same time we are only getting prices from one-half up to two-thirds of what, according to those prices, we ought to receive. (Cheers.) It does not stop there. It does not even stop at fair dealing, but it goes beyond that. The other day I met in the train a gentleman who is a large landowner in the West, and whose veracity is quite unimpeachable, and he told me that he had lately met a man who boasted openly that he had made £200,000 last year by buying Canadian beef and selling it as prime English. Now, gentlemen, I say that is neither free trade nor fair trade, but it is unfair trade. (Cheers.) (*See page 59.*)

Foreign and Colonial Meat to be Labelled.

Those gains I distinctly brand as fraudulent. That is what they are (cheers), and one of the very first things that we propose to do, therefore, is to bring in a Bill, and I have reason to believe that it will be supported from both sides of both Houses, in order to make it compulsory to label colonial and foreign meat. (Loud cheers.) That is one of those very few things which will benefit everybody all round, except the person who does not run fair and square. It will benefit the consumer first of all, because he will know then that if he gives 9d., 10d., or 11d. a pound for beef, he is not having foreign beef palmed off upon him as English. It will benefit the producer, because when we bring our English meat into the market, and find, as I trust we always shall, honest English men and women to whom a penny a pound is neither here nor there, but who would rather buy English beef because it is a good thing for English agriculture, we shall be able to sell it for a decent price, and that will benefit the producer. But there is another person whom, oddly enough, it will benefit, and that is the honest butcher in provincial towns. How is that? Well, my butcher tells me this. I have known him for years, and I know that he always sells and professes to sell English beef. He said to me, "What happens? Every market day two or three men come into the market, and bring some horrible foreign stuff. I know that it is foreign, but the people here do not. Those men sell the meat for twopence a pound less than I can afford to sell mine at. They sell it as prime English beef, and they drain off my customers, and the next day a number of my customers come to me and say, ' Why cannot you sell us beef at the same price as we can get it in the market ? ' " For this reason I say that the honest dealer in the towns will welcome such a measure, because it will enable him to brand the man who comes into the market and sells foreign meat as if it were English grown. (Cheers.)

There are two other classes whom it will also benefit. It will benefit the producer of foreign meat. I happen to know that in our Colonies at this moment they are asking for exactly such a bill as we propose, simply because the butchers who buy the Colonial meat and sell it again as English keep it off the market which would really buy it. They do not let the poor people get a chance of it, and therefore the New Zealand people, or the Queensland people, or whoever they are who send it, can only send the small quantity of it, which will command a high price here, and they cannot send those quantities of it which the poor people in England want, and would consume if they could get it. And, finally, it will benefit the labouring class, because at the present moment a great quantity of the foreign meat which comes to this country is so manipulated that they cannot get it except at a high price. If the measure is passed, if the poor man wants to get cheap meat, and if his necessities make him obliged to get cheap meat, he will be able to do so, and that will be an enormous benefit to him. Therefore I say that if you can do something—and by organising you may do much—in the direction of reducing our local taxation, and if you can do something—and much you may do—in the direction of stopping, not the fair profit, but the fraudulent profit of the middleman which now comes between your profit and loss, you will have done a great deal to justify the existence of the National Agricultural Union, and whatever you spend to bring it about will be money well invested. (Cheers.)

Protection and Free Trade.

There are other points, of course, which are not to be found in the progamme. I have made at the outset a concession to human nature which I know is strong everywhere, particularly in Yorkshire. You will find in the programme that, although members are bound to co-operate for their common good, there is nothing whatever to prevent any member making with his fellow-member any bargain he pleases when he is selling him a horse, so that that noble animal can still continue, even between chief friends, to act as a kind of safety valve for our predatory instincts. (Laughter.) But there are other things which are not to be found in our programme, and after what I have said you will not be surprised that they are not to be found there. Let me remind you again that, so far as I am concerned here and now, our programme can only consist of those points upon which we are agreed, and I have no power—and it would be a breach of faith on my part if I were to do so—to introduce into that programme any point, no matter how important, upon which we disagree. The first point, of course, which will rise to your minds with regard to this question is the question of Protection. (Cheers.) Of course, as Lord Herries has clearly pointed out, I have no title whatever to impose my individual opinion upon the Union ; but perhaps at this moment, as it may have some fictitious, or, rather, adventitious weight, owing to the scheme being connected with my name, I ought to tell you what my own opinion upon that point is if you desire that I should do so. (Hear, hear, and cheers.)

Within the limits of a speech, already I fear too long—(" No, no," and cheers)—it is impossible for me to go into that great question as fully as I should like to do; but my own convictions upon it remain precisely what they were in 1880, when I stood for the Borough of Newark, and what I said then I say now—that I believe, myself, in universal Free Trade if you can get it; and, as a means of getting it, and for many other Imperial reasons, I believe that the true solution, and the eventual solution, towards which the people of this country and of our Colonies ought to work, is a great Imperial federation. In passing I may point out that the question of Protection and Free Trade, which seems to be one that divides us so exactly, is not really a question of principle at all, but simply, in my opinion, a matter of business. Many people suppose that it is as wrong not to believe in Free Trade as it would be not to go to church; but I think that if that is the case we are a very wicked people in this country. Let anybody who likes take an acre of his own land, and let him plant it with tobacco, and let him try to sell the tobacco in this country. He will be fined heavily, and if he does not pay the fine he will have an opportunity of meditating in gaol on the question whether this is a Free Trade country or not. (Laughter and cheers.)

Tea Duty.

There are one or two things which, whether as Free Trader or Protectionist, I have never been able to see. If we do impose taxes upon imports—and, wounding as it may be to the conscience of Free Traders, we cannot deny that we do, and it wounds my conscience as a Free Trader—why, in the name of heaven and common sense, can we not impose them upon something which would do good to the producers in this country, instead of imposing them upon articles like tea and things of that class which do producers here no good at all? Not a single English acre, not a single English labourer, is or can be employed in growing tea, and therefore the duty which is paid upon the tea is simply so much out of the consumer's pocket without being of the slightest benefit to anybody. It is nonsense to talk about tea being a luxury. It is almost as much a necessity even to working men in these days as his daily bread. Therefore you are taxing a necessary of life, and you are taxing it in such a foolish manner as to do no good whatever to the class at home whom you might benefit without the least harm to the consumer, or taking a farthing out of his pocket, if you took the tax off tea, and put it on something which we do grow in this country. (Cheers.)

The Beer Duty.

Well, there is another question—I fear that you will think me very dense indeed that I cannot see my way through these things more clearly than I do—There is the question of the beer duty. Beer pays a duty of six shillings and threepence per barrel, and that duty, so far as I can see. benefits no producer in the country. Why could not the duty be arranged in such a way as to ensure that beer should be made of English barley and hops? (Loud and continued cheers.) It would add a great deal to your income and to mine. It would take nothing whatever out of the pocket of the consumer, and I am perfectly certain that the beer which he would receive would agree very much better with his interior economy.

You will, observe, of course, that these are questions on which as a Free Trader I am trying to arrange my tariffs again—those tariffs which I have already insisted on imposing. I think these are matters which will form the ground of much comment and useful argument between the members of this Union, whether theoretically they be Free Traders or Protectionists, when they join it. But let me say this, that if I were the most ardent

Protectionist in this room I should do exactly what I am doing now. And why should I do it? For this reason; and let me commend this to the attention of Protectionists all over the country. Suppose I wanted to place a duty on this or that article of food. I should find that the labouring classes were against me. Odd though it may appear to a Protectionist, they do like cheap food. They say that a tax imposed would very likely raise—almost certainly raise—the price of their food, because we have not yet had the opportunity of teaching them by our Co-operative Union that the price of bread varies very little—not half as much as it ought to do with the price of corn. Rightly or wrongly, they believe that the price of their food would be raised; and, rightly or wrongly, they do not believe that if they were to assist you in placing any such duty upon corn, they would receive a corresponding equivalent in the form of higher wages. (Cheers.)

A Sliding Scale of Wages.

Now, particularly in these days of education, the labouring man is as able to do a sum as well as you or I. If you could prove to him that he would get four or five shillings a-week more wages, and that his bread bill would be only sixpence a-week more, he would be quite capable, not only of doing an addition sum, but of doing a subtraction sum, and he would take the sixpence from the 3s. or 4s., and he would see that 2s. 6d. or 3s. 6d. a week would be left to him as clear profit. (Cheers.) That matter was touched at the very root by the Ex-Minister of Agriculture, who, I am very glad to think, is in sympathy with us in this movement, although he believes that we ought to use the existing organisations—a point which I shall come to directly, and on which I may say at this moment I am quite in sympathy with him. He touched this point at the very root when he stated what a labourer said to him—and I see one or two labourers here, and I know that they will understand this point. What the labourer said was, "Who will give us a lease of them better wages?" Well, I will tell you: the National Agricultural Union. Suppose that now we were to do what the right honourable gentleman, Mr. Lowther—(cheers)—who so ably and impartially presided at the Conference, has proposed. The proposal was one that I supported myself about six years ago at Lincoln. It was to have a sliding scale of wages according to the price of agricultural produce. At the present moment one farmer may adopt it and another farmer may say, "No, I know nothing about your sliding scale;" but I think that the Agricultural Union might adopt a sliding scale of wages on quite different grounds, because, as I pointed out, the labourers are partners in the business of agriculture. They expect to take a share in its fall, and they are now doing it; and they expect, and they have a right to expect, a corresponding share in its rise. Now, I say that if a Union composed of landlords, tenants, and labourers were to adopt the policy of a sliding scale of wages, there would be the "lease of those wages" that the labourers want.

After having told you that I am myself a universal Free Trader, I am now pointing out from a Protectionist's point of view what an excellent weapon would be put into his hands by the Union, supposing that by argument he were able to capture it, and that is the way in which great victories are won in this country. We have a large mass of our fellow citizens, and we want to persuade them, just as I want to persuade you, of what I believe to be a great truth. Well, we go to meetings, we have a division after full discussion; the majority rules, and the minority loyally bows to its decision. After the Union is established we shall have free discussion. Free Traders, Protectionists, mono-metallists, bi-metallists, tri-metallists, if there are such people, can bring forward their various remedies. When once we get the Union formed they will have an excellent opportunity of persuading those who are members of it of the truth of what they say; and, although we may adopt a sliding scale of wages on other grounds, let me point out to our Protectionist friends what an enormous advantage they would gain by a side issue if the National Union were to adopt a sliding scale of wages, as I hope it will do. (Cheers.)

Now, my lords and gentlemen, I feel that I have really trespassed upon you for a quite unconscionable length of time; but we are here on what may prove to be a great historical occasion, and let us not grudge the necessary time for going to the roots of this matter; and if I appear to labour it, do remember that although you represent here the whole of the North of England, the enormous body of your constituents are out of doors, and that in many cases they have not heard and do not know as much about this scheme as you do, and it is for them, if not for you, that I venture to go into some detail.

I have got as far in the programme I think as telling you what are the great objects aimed at, and what are the general principles on which these objects are to be obtained. I think that probably you will desire that I should explain as shortly as I can, though in some detail, how we propose to carry out those objects.

Procedure.

You will remember that the Union by its constitution is to be representative of every class; that its central offices are to be in London; and that it is to have branches, of course, in every part of the country. The way in which it is proposed to work, that is one which is quite familiar to those who, like myself, belong to the Central and Associated Chambers of Agriculture; and as I know that this meeting is desirous, as your chairman, Lord Herries, has suggested to me, that I should define my attitude with regard to existing organisations and the Agricultural Union, I will take this opportunity of doing it.

Chambers of Agriculture.

Let me point out to you that there never was a greater mistake made than was made by a gentleman at the Cheshire Chamber—I think his name was Mr. Tibbald—who stated that I had taken action in this matter outside the Central Chamber. The Conference at which I proposed this Union was summoned by the Central Chamber of Agriculture. I am myself a member of the Lincoln Chamber, and I frequently attend the meetings of the Central Chamber; and, not only so, but my own proposition, the draft scheme which I suomitted to you, is to be officially submitted to the organising committee of that Conference, all the members of which are members of the Central Chamber of Agriculture. And not only so, but here I take the opportunity of expressing in the warmest way my personal acknowledgment to Mr. Clay for seconding that proposal; and a more distinguished member of the Central Chamber there is not than Mr. Clay. I also take this opportunity of doing the same with regard to Mr. Rew, the Secretary of the Central Chamber of Agriculture, who has worked indefatigably, almost night and day with me, in bringing this matter to the point at which we have now arrived. (Cheers.) It is not because he is not loyal to the Central Chamber, for a more loyal servant to the Central Chamber does not exist; but it is because he believes that the objects which we have in view are one and the same, and that we shall shortly arrive together at the means of carrying them out.

Yorkshire Union.

Not only that, but this meeting itself which I have the honour of addressing has been called together very much by the exertions of the chairman of the Yorkshire Union of Farmers' Clubs, Dr. Wright. (Cheers.) There again I have relied upon existing organisations. So far from being hostile to them, I welcome them and recognise this fact—and no one who is here will deny it—that in every interest—in the agricultural interest perhaps more than any other—there are only certain people who will come forward and do the work. We cannot spare these people. The Central and Associated Chambers of Agriculture contain some of the most eminent practical agriculturists in the kingdom. It would be perfectly suicidal to the Union if it were to put forward for a moment the plea that it could do without such men as those, many of whom I see around me, and others whom I often meet at the Central Chamber of Agriculture. But at the same time it is no secret that the Central Chamber itself has had before it, and has, I believe, favourably received, a proposal for a change of name, and, if I am right, the Business Committee have adopted the proposal. Well, I think that that is very opportune to our present discussion.

Popularising the "Chambers."

It appears to me also to be generally recognised in the country now, that it would be a very wise thing to allow labourers to enter these Chambers of Agriculture. I do not know whether I read the Press of the country aright, but at the present moment I must say that the National Agricultural Union occupies a far larger field of the public eye than the Central and Associated Chambers of Agriculture. You must remember that this scheme has not been and cannot be officially discussed by any organisations except existing Chambers and Farmers' Clubs, and therefore if there was any leaning of opinion in those bodies it would naturally be in the direction of reserving themselves until they saw whether a new organisation was about to be placed by the side of theirs ; and I quite accept it as an excellent thing that they should do so. As business men they know two things. First, that it is of no use to go twice over the same ground; and, secondly, that the tenant farmers at the present moment, and perhaps others, are unable to afford two sets of subscriptions. I quite recognise that fact. At the present moment I have thrown myself warmly, as it were, into the arms of the existing organisations. Less than that, I think, cannot be said by anybody who is connected with them. I have not in any way indicated any want of trust in them, or in their discussion and consideration of the matter. On the contrary, I think that it was at my proposal that the scheme was sent down by the Central Chamber to every Associated Chamber and Farmers' Club in the kingdom for their consideration. I asked Mr. Rew specially— and many others here will bear me out when I say it, for they must have seen it—to add at the bottom of his letter a postscript from myself to this effect : " Lord Winchilsea desires me to add that he believes that we shall find in your organisation an admirable weapon for carrying out the scheme. ' (Cheers.)

What will Happen.

But now, gentlemen, with regard to exactly what will happen. We might, of course, even at the present moment, be content with knowing that we are travelling together amicably along the same road, towards the same goal. Some Chambers of Agriculture, in fact, have not been able to be restrained. The Maidstone Chamber of Agriculture has formed itself into a " branch of the National Agricultural Union," so that there is now a branch without a tree—(laughter)—and other associations are doing the same thing. Well, they are all quite right. I may venture to prophesy —it is never a very safe thing to do—that what I think will happen will be this: The Central Chamber of Agriculture and the Associated Chambers of Agriculture recognise, apparently, two things, neither of which, perhaps, came from myself, but from their own inner consciousness. One is that the name which they bear does not command much enthusiasm in the country; and the other is that, since the admission of the agricultural labourer to the franchise, the basis on which they act must be popularised if it is to have any considerable weight in public opinion. (Cheers.)

Dissolution.

We in England act very much according to constitutional precedent, and we have an admirable one set for us, I think, with regard to this matter. Does not the position very much resemble the position that Parliament finds itself in when it has passed a Reform Bill extending the franchise. The Central Chamber of Agriculture are in that position. They mean to extend their franchise, to admit others to it. Very well, what does Parliament do under such circumstances ? Why, directly it finds that new constituencies exist, and that it does not, therefore, any longer continue to represent the whole of the electors of the country, it at once dissolves. There is a general election, and Parliament reappears in a new and extended form, as soon as the elections can be held. I think that something of that kind will probably take place with regard to the Central and Associated Chambers of Agriculture. I may say that at the present moment I am not entitled to speak for them, for I do not know what their decision may be, but nothing, if I can possibly avoid it, will induce me to take any action which would necessitate the Union dispensing with the services of those who have served the Chambers of Agriculture so well in the time past. But, as I have said before, it will be impossible to put the contents of a soup tureen into a teacup. If these organisations will not popularise themselves, you cannot confine the National Agricultural Union within their limits. Their wisdom, I think, will be to adapt themselves to existing circumstances, and they will find in me, both as a loyal member of those Chambers, and also as one intensely interested in the success of this movement, a co-operator to the greatest extent which they can desire.

There are only one or two more points upon which I should like to speak to you, and for which I must crave your indulgence for one moment.

Payment of Delegates.

The draft scheme is before you, of course, in the form in which it was originally sent out. There are two modifications which I should like at the proper moment to suggest. One is—and I think that you will see that it is a just one—that the delegates should be entitled, as indeed they are at the Central Chamber, to be paid their expenses when they attend meetings of the branches, and of the Central Council; and also, in the case of labourers, their day's wages as well. It is a mockery, of course, to give representation to a class which you know cannot afford to pay for itself the expenses of attending the gathering which it has been elected to attend.

Three Delegates.

Then I think that it would be an excellent emendation that we should elect three delegates instead of one, and that there should be one delegate from each class of which the Union is composed. I only foreshadow that now, but it is of great importance, I think, because it will assure that in every place, and even at the Central Council itself, each of these three classes is neither over nor under-represented. That is a distinction of importance that I have made in the draft scheme, and I take this, the first public opportunity that I have had of bringing it forward.

Future Aims.

There are many other points with which a great organisation like this, if it is successful, may be expected to deal. It would form an admirable means of insuring your cattle, for instance, and the pigs of poor men and others, against fatalities and disease. The number of members which the Union would contain would insure you at very low rates. The same may be said, I think, with regard to a question which has been for many years a very interesting one to myself—the subject brought forward originally by Canon Blackley. I mean the question of pensions and sick pay. Now, I think that we might, in an immense association like that, do very much by contributions from all the members of it to assist the labouring members to have old age pensions and sick pay. (Cheers.) When Canon Blackley brought forward his scheme he used to call me his first lieutenant; and I went over the country to many meetings, and I never had anything but a unanimous vote in favour of such a proposal.

There are other things, of course, which the Union might do, but they are in the dim and distant future; and as this is a practical meeting, I would ask you to consider only that which is, or may be fairly said to be in the present. I have endeavoured to lay before you—though I fear I have done so imperfectly—what in my humble opinion is the nature of the crisis; what is the combination by which alone it can be adequately met; what are the means by which that combination can be carried out; and what are the items which should, and the items which should not, at present appear upon its programme. So far, of course, I have treated of what may be called our commercial interests. I have stated that they are all one, and I desire once more to lay down this principle before I conclude—that the Union must be one between all classes for the advancement of their common interests; for pressing forward all the objects upon which we are agreed; and for diminishing by discussion those on which we differ.

Moral Aspect of the Union.

But before I leave the matter, as I do with the greatest confidence, in your hands, you will allow me for one moment to indicate to you what I think is even a higher point of view. History and experience teach us—do they not?—that in the long run the prosperity of a nation depends not upon any accidental circumstances of soil or climate, but essentially upon those great qualities of head and heart which enable one fellow-citizen to work with another, and all to work together for the common good. (Cheers.) Are we not dangerously drifting away from this position in England—nay, to come nearer home, in our own industry? (A voice, "Yes.") A gentle-

c

man says " Yes," and it is the answer of the conscience of this meeting to the question which I ask.

And do we not sometimes feel misgivings when, as we walk along the street and pass a labourer, he does not give us the accustomed frank salutation, but, perhaps, looks away ? Perhaps, too, we know that he is taking counsel with others who are not of us, and that he is lending a not unwilling ear when they tell him that his interests are different from our own. And does not conscience whisper to you and to me, with our greater knowledge, and our ampler opportunities of instructing him in the past, that we are " Verily guilty concerning our brother ?·" (Cheers.) If that be so, may I entreat you, before it be too late, to infuse something of the old harmonious spirit into the relations between one class and another by means of this National Agricultural Union ; if it be yet in time to avert that decree of fate which seems to menace us with some great national crisis, as the punishment of our unhappy divisions, in the not remote future.

We may succeed, or we may fail, but it will be a noble enterprise. At least we may go forward with high courage and confident hopes, and inasmuch as in this matter we seek not to injure the interests of another, but simply to defend our own—to unite, and not to divide—(Cheers), we may claim not only the sympathy of our fellow-men, but that higher approval without which even the most indispensable of national industries, and the most perfect of human organisations, are foredoomed to wither and decay. (Loud cheers).   W.

SPEECH

BY THE
EARL OF WINCHILSEA & NOTTINGHAM

*Delivered at a Meeting of Agriculturists, held in the Lecture Hall,
Tower Street, Ipswich, on Tuesday, January 17th, 1893.*

CAPTAIN E. G. PRETYMAN IN THE CHAIR.

THE EARL OF WINCHILSEA AND NOTTINGHAM: Mr. Chairman, my Lords, Ladies and Gentlemen, I have to thank you very much for the kind way in which you have greeted the introduction of myself by your Chairman, because it shows that, whether you think that I am mistaken and my enterprise about to fail or not, still you do give me credit for sincerity in this matter (Cheers.) And, if we start upon the discussion of my scheme on this ground, I have no fear that before this meeting ends I shall be able to show you that it is of real practical utility.

I am glad this meeting is held at Ipswich, for in this Union we are far from doing anything which would injure the towns of this country in their trade; we from the very first claim them as engaged in sister industries with our own. Now here in Ipswich, where does the mainspring of your commercial prosperity lie? Everybody who knows Ipswich knows that one of your greatest industries—perhaps your greatest industry here—is the making of agricultural implements. What town, therefore, is more interested than Ipswich in the prosperity of agriculture? When I say that eight millions of rural population are interested in this question, I understate it very much, because there are towns all over England like Ipswich which are as much interested really in agriculture as are the three classes who are more directly engaged in it.

"A Great Surging Cry."

I noticed a letter this morning in the *East Anglian Daily Times*—and let me say in passing that it is a great comfort, when one is addressing large meetings in every part of the country, to get to a town where there is a good daily paper. I do not know why it is, but I always find more intelligent audiences, people more able to grasp the leading topics of the day, when that is the case, than when I go to places where no such organ exists. The letter to which I refer was this. It says, "The report of the meeting to be held to-day will be read with the keenest interest by tens of thousands to-morrow." And again, "Whose interests are they which are to be dealt with to-day? Thank God, not one class only, but all classes—landlords, farmers, tradesmen, small shopkeepers, village shoemakers, labourers, yes, even their wives and daughters and their sisters, too." I say, gentlemen, thank God that so many people all over the country are beginning to find it out. That is what really fills me with thankfulness, that, wherever I go and wherever I expose this scheme to the public eye, there follows a great surging cry behind me, "That is the thing for the country. We must pull together if we are to save England from going down the hill." (Cheers.)

Now, let us approach the subject from that point of view, but also from a very practical one. I have announced—and I mean to make good what I have said—that my remarks to-day, although, of course, it will be my duty to place before you the scheme and the circumstances under which I introduce it, are to be directed especially to agricultural labourers. I am, therefore, very glad to see that so many of them have been able, even in this inclement weather, to accept my invitation. (Cheers.) And I come to them here not to make them a speech, but to talk to them as one man to another, and I ask them to follow me carefully and to see as I go on whether I make good what I shall say from the very start in answer to a question which has been asked me.

The Labourer's Share.

Now, I have been asked this: Supposing that the labourers join in this scheme for bringing back prosperity to agriculture, what security have they that they will get their fair share of the profits when we get them? Now, I believe that if the labourers of this country knew that they were absolutely certain to get fourpence out of every shilling, which the two other classes got when any rise took place in the great industry they are connected with, they would join us heart and soul. But they ask the question before they go into it, "Are we, or are we not, absolutely safe and secure that we shall not be in the position that we were in the last time agriculture was prosperous, when we did have corn of all kinds at a good price, but when we did not have our proper rise in wages in consequence?" Gentlemen, I admit that most fully, and I do say to you that this is the great central idea of everything that I am going to tell you, and I beg you to keep it, as it were, in your mind, and apply it to everything I say—that in this matter I treat all the three classes as partners, equal partners in one great business. What is the result of that? Why, that each partner is entitled to receive an equal share of the profits of the business in which he engages; that, if the profits go up, each class must share in them alike. Very well, then, we will start with that central idea as the answer to the question.

And you will ask me now, how do I mean to carry that out? Well, that will be clear to you as we go on with the scheme; but I ask any labourer in this room if I do not make perfectly clear, as I go on, how what I say is going to benefit him, just to say, "Well, I do not quite see that point," and I will make it clear if I can.

No Party Politics.

First of all, I ask you, are we going to play with this great question or not? Are we really in such a position that something must be done? I think that there can be very little question about that. However important other questions may be, to my mind there is none which touches in importance at the present moment the condition of agriculture. We have heard of, party politics, and I have been told that it was a great pity to put my intimate friend, Mr. Pretyman, in the chair here, because he is the Conservative candidate. I say, yes, this has nothing to do with party politics at all. But that does not mean that all party people are to keep out of it. It means that both parties are to come into it, and, therefore, I am as glad to see my friend occupying the chair here as I am to see on the platform by the side of him the gentleman who is now your member and will be his opponent. (Cheers.)

I myself have a keen eye to business, and I know perfectly well that when I get the candidates on the one side and on the other both equally pledged to the Union, I may leave this division alone, because whoever gets in, the National Agricultural Union's interests are safe. I should, indeed, be sorry to see them both away. I am glad to see them both here. At the next meeting I hold, if 1 can manage it, I shall have the Radical member in the chair, and his Conservative opponent sitting next to him, both drinking in the same truths, and both ready, when they get to the House of Commons, to carry them out; and then I shall turn my back on them. I shall say, " Gentlemen, you both seem to me very good fellows. I wish you both success, and I hope you will both get in." (Laughter.)

Well, I see that a newspaper has made the following calculation, that if I am successful I shall get 400 members in the House of Commons. Well, that is a large order, gentlemen, but still I do not say at all that that newspaper is not correct, and if 1 can do in every constituency what I have done in this one—get the Conservative and the Radical candidates both on the same platform, one to take the chair and the other to propose a resolution in favour of my scheme—I shall get, not 400, but 660 members of the House of Commons in favour of the scheme. (Laughter.) What I should like to do at the present moment is this. I should like to go up respectfully, both to the present and to the past Prime Minister of England, take them both by the hand and lead them into a comfortable room together : I should lock the door of that room, and I should say, " Gentlemen, I will let you out when you have made up your minds together that agriculture is the first thing that you have to attend to, both of you." (Laughter.) I should say, if 1 might, " The British Constitution has lasted us a thousand years. Depend upon it, it will last another two years without any trouble on your part ; but remember that there are thousands of acres of land without any labourers on them ; there are thousands of poor fellows without wages, without food, and without clothing. These are the questions you ought, both of you, first of all to grapple with, and to impress upon your followers, as I am impressing upon them, on both sides of me, here and now, that it is their first duty to the State, to take them up."

That is what I mean by this not being a party political meeting. I mean that both the great parties in the State are to take agriculture up equally, and are to take it up as in duty bound, because they profess to be promoting the interests of this great country ; and I can show them by such statistics as they cannot deny that its interests at this moment centre and pivot on the great industry by which you and I are engaged in earning our livelihood.

"Did you ever think of the labouring man before?"

Well, gentlemen, of course there are many of you here who are inclined to ask yourselves a question which I shall think it my duty to answer. You may be very much in the position which I am told by my hostess at York her little boy of three years found himself in when I went to stay with them. He said to his mother, "I am very much disappointed with Lord Winchilsea." Well, after the comments that have been made upon me in the public Press, I am humble enough to expect anything ; but still I wanted to know why, and his mother said to me, "I asked him why, and he answered, ' Of course I expected Lord Winchilsea to come here in a full suit of armour.' " Well, gentlemen, I came here without any armour at all. I came only with that breastplate of sincerity which we have heard of in the old writer which we used to learn at our mother's knee. That is how I came to you, armed with nothing but truth and sincerity, and desirous to do my best for this cause.

But you may say this to me, and very fairly, "We admit the crisis. We admit we are all down as low almost as we can get. Many remedies have been proposed, but none seems to meet the case. If you come before your fellow-citizens with a project for altering this state of things, and if you offer to lead us in a particular direction which you say will conduct us to prosperity, we have a right to ask you this question : Did you ever think of us labouring men before we had a vote at all ? Did you ever do anything to help us before that time ?" Gentlemen, I am ready for the question. I court any inquiry you like to make as to what has been my past in connection with the labourers of this country ; and as I know you are all too good-natured to ask me the question, I will ask it myself, and for a few moments only I will trouble you with the answer to it.

When I first entered political life I chose as the constituency I wished to represent one which contained a great number of agricultural labourers. I was told that I could not get in there, because there was not a single landlord who lived in that division. I said, "Never mind. I have lived among agri-cultural labourers all my life. They know me, and I know them. I will go there, and try whether I cannot, off my own bat, as we say in cricket, win that division." I went, and I won that division, and I represented from that moment in the House of Commons more agricultural labourers, I believe, than any member of that House, and it was one of the things I was most proud to do. Then at the end of that Parliament, when I was not well enough to go back and contest that seat again, they asked me to sit again, and, though I was not present there—and, you know, in election matters those who are absent are always in the wrong—I was returned again by a majority three times as great in my absence as they had formerly given me when I was there to defend myself. I am entitled to be proud of that, and I am proud of it.

Labour Delegates.

It did not quite end there, because what did I do ? What was my record in the House of Commons ? Well, I saw this—and I wonder that a great many people have not seen it too—that in a large agricultural constituency, composed of villages scattered all over the place, we cannot get the opinion of the agricultural labourers upon any Act of Parliament that is going to be passed by going round to the villages, because while I was going round to the villages the Act would have been passed, you know, while I was away. What I said to them was this : "Will you in every polling district elect a delegate to confer with me on every great question when I summon you together?" I said, "I do not care a bit whether he is a Conservative or a Radical, but elect the man you listen to at your clubs or at the public-house, and let him come to me. When there is a great question affecting your interests I will call them all together, and we will have a talk about it."

Allotment Bill.

Now, what happened? At that moment an Allotment Bill was the great question before the country. As soon as the Bill was printed I sent it to my agricultural labourer delegates to read. They came to meet me at Boston, forty of them, some of them being as great Radicals as—I was going to say, as I am myself. But, however, a great many of them were great Radicals. Well, they came there, and we went through that Bill, clause by clause, from beginning to end. The labourers themselves, knowing of course a great deal about the subject of allotments, made several most sensible suggestions as we went on. I took them down on paper. There were one or two labourers who tried to get a little off the point and make a little political capital, but the others would not have it. They said,

"Question, question," and they would not hear it. They went through that Bill with me in a business-like way, and the result was this. At the end of the meeting I said, "Gentlemen, you have done more business in two hours than the House of Commons has done in three weeks. I congratulate you on being by far the most business-like assembly of the two." But it did not end there. I happened the next day to see the Prime Minister, and I said, "Now, as this is a Bill that is going to interest agricultural labourers, would you like to know what they think about it?" He said, "I should, very much." I put before him those alterations which these labourers' delegates had suggested to me, and in more than one case he adopted them and put them into the Bill, and there they are at this moment. A labourer said to me after that, "Well, here is the sort of man we want to represent us. He calls us together to give our opinion. In twenty-four hours he is up with the Prime Minister. Twelve hours afterwards he puts it into the Act. That is what I call business." (Laughter.)

Allotments Compensation Act.

But, gentlemen, it did not end there. You will think that I am never going to end, I am afraid. A little later on, Sir Edward Birkbeck, who is a good friend of yours, and who, I am proud to say, is a great personal friend of mine, said to me, "Why should we not introduce a Bill into the House of Commons giving the agricultural labourer the same compensation for his improvements on his allotment when he is turned out of it, or leaves it of his own accord, as tenants have on the farms?" Well," I said, "with all my heart. I think he ought to have it." He said, "Will you draw a Bill yourself?" You see that I have to do a little of everything. I said, "Yes, I will." He said, "The whole thing is that it must not cost them a farthing." "Well," I said, "if it is an Act that is going to do that, it is the first Act of Parliament that I ever heard of that can be carried out without costing anybody anything." But I drew the Bill. It is an Act now. By that Act you can now get compensation when you are turned out of your allotment, and, gentlemen, it is the only Act of Parliament on the Statute Book that can be carried out for absolutely nothing. We passed it through the House of Commons by a very curious trick, because of the opposition of the Irish members. I should like to tell you about that if I had time; but it so happened that, much to my own regret, I was obliged to go at that moment to the House of Lords, and directly I found myself on my legs there I took the Bill up again, and I passed it through the House of Lords as well as through the House of Commons. Now, that is a thing which I think has never happened to anybody before. The result of it is that you have now got compensation for your allotments.

Lord Winchilsea's Own Allotments.

Well, now, why did I do all that? Because I had been doing it for years before on my own estates; because I know perfectly well that, although the labourers look, and I think rightly, to good wages and to permanent work and employment as the mainstay of their prosperity in life, a labourer has got a good deal that is valuable besides what he can get in that way. He has got spare time. Now a labourer's spare time is his spare capital, and as he knows a great deal about the land—a good deal more about it than some farmers, including myself, do—he naturally says "That spare time I should like to employ upon the land on my own account." Well, I say with all my heart, "Why in the world should he not do so?" Gentlemen, it is a wonderful thing how many people have wanted to give you allotments, especially out of other people's land, ever since you have had a vote. (Laughter.) But the labourers had allotments on my estates years and years before they had a vote, and not only that, but they have had them at very much the same rent that I should have charged a farmer for the same land.

How to Climb the Ladder.

Not only that. I do not think that the labourers of this country will ever be in the position in which they ought to be as long as they have only wages and only allotments. I have been trying for years on my own property with some success to carry it a step further. Now, we all know that in every class—it is the same in mine, and it is the same in yours—there are certain men who want to get on. They say, "I have been born in this position, but is that any reason why I should always stay in it? I will climb up if I can get something to catch hold of. I will climb a bit higher." Well, I say that there is no greater pleasure to a man in my position than to be able to set that man's foot on the first round of the ladder that will lead him up to independence. (Cheers.)

Now, I will tell you how I have done that on my property, because when I say that I have done it there, you may know that I want the same thing done all over the country, and I can see my way to get it done. What I have done is this: I know quite well that there is only one time in a man's life, whether he is rich or poor, when he can save any money, and that is before he is married. (Laughter.) I do not mean the slightest reflection upon the other sex. (Laughter.) [A voice: "Money is not everything."] My friend says that "money is not everything." No, that is perfectly true, but it is something, and if you want to take a hundred acres of land, to have saved a little money is a good deal, if it is not everything. You know the real fact is this: that if a labouring man is married and has got six or seven children, he cannot save much money after that, but if he is a single man in service, and is getting the same wages before he marries as he is afterwards when he is married and has got several children, well, he can save something out of that if you show him that by the self-denial necessary to do it he will get something at the end of it. Now, our people in Lincolnshire—I do not know whether you use the same expression here, but if you ask them if they can save money after they are married and have got a family, they say, "Oh no, I have got too many ankle biters for that job." But before they are married in my part of the world, and when they are in service, they can and do put by a certain amount.

"Cow Cottages."

Now what happens? When a man like that is ready for it I find him a cottage with five or six or seven acres of grass land to it. And there, I say, I do put his foot on to that first rung of the ladder. I have labourers in my village at home who have cow cottages, as we call them. That is to say, they start, perhaps, with four or five or six acres of grass land. They come to me and they say, "We have saved some money to buy the stock. Will you give us a cottage?" I say "Yes." In a few years after a larger cottage, perhaps, with ten acres of land is vacant. Then they apply to me for that and I let them have it, and so they mount up stage by stage until at last I have men who work for daily wages and who farm as much as twenty-five or twenty-six acres of grass land.

Well, now, I say that that, I think, is a fair, good, honest attempt to raise the labourers of this country, partly by their own endeavours and partly by what it is a pleasure to one to be able to do, from the condition of merely gaining wages to the condition of an honest independence. And there is this about it which I ought to say is a sort of pendant to what I said just now about people not being able to save money after they are married—that the whole kernel of the thing is this: that they work for daily wages on the farms, and that their wives and sisters manage the stock and the dairy entirely. (Cheers.) I think that that is a state of things which you, as labourers, all of you might desire to aspire to. I desire that you should; and I think that the Agricultural Union, if you join it, may be able to help you very much in that direction. At any rate, gentlemen, whether you think so or not, I do say that I have given a fair answer to the question which might be put to me, "Is this the first time you have ever thought of laying your hand to the work of helping us?" I say, no, it is not, because for years I have been trying to do my part. (Cheers.)

What is the "N.A.U."?

Now, what is the scheme which I want to place before you as practical men? Nobody will deny that we want something, because we are all, I think, in as bad a condition as it is possible for us to be. Something must be done. The question is, What? Nobody has proposed anything to which we can all agree, except the proposal that I have placed before the country. That is absolutely the case. Let anybody get up who likes to follow me, and say that there is any other scheme which all agriculturists could combine upon, except mine. He may say it, but I shall be very much surprised if he is able to prove it. Therefore, at any rate, I think we ought to give it a very fair and a very searching consideration, and see whether it is the thing we want, or whether it is not. Let me go back for a moment to the promise that I made you at the beginning. You will find in this scheme, as labourers—and I address you more particularly—that your interests are made safe in this way, that you are treated as partners with the other two interests in the land. So, whatever rise they get you get.

Well, now, how do I do that? First of all, as you know, in the letter which I had the honour to address to you, the labourers of England, I promised you that you should have your fair share and voice and control in the management of the National Agricultural Union. That is of great importance to you, because, if this is going to be a great engine to work out certain things for our good, you ought to see that you have your fair share and control over the management of it. Now, how is that going to be done? Well, first of all, the Union itself is to be composed of members of all the three classes interested in agriculture. They are to be joined together in one great Union to promote their common interests and they are to press forward all those questions upon which they are agreed; and, fortunately, there are a great many of very great interest to us upon which we are agreed, because I have put them in the programme, and no agriculturist has seriously attacked them. That is a great thing to start with.

How it is to be Worked Out?

Now, how is the thing going to be worked out in detail? As I tell you, we shall have a Central Council in London, and we shall start our branch councils in parishes. Now why do I do that? Because I know quite well that a working man cannot walk into a town every time he wants to attend a meeting. He must have one in his own parish if he is really to be represented. (A laugh.) A gentleman laughs, but does he mean to have a meeting in his own house? I say in his own parish. Every labourer, surely, who takes an interest in these questions can attend a meeting held in his own parish, if it is held at such a time of day that he can attend it. It should be held in the evening, of course, after work is done, when you can all attend meetings. The first branches we shall found will be those in parishes.

Equal Delegates.

Every branch will be obliged to elect three delegates, one landowner, one occupier, and one labourer; so that you see there you get an equal representation of all classes. Those three delegates will represent that particular parish or village at a council, which will be held at the market town, because that is the easiest place to get to next. Therefore, the market town branch, you see, will be composed of equal parts of landowners, tenants, and labourers, one of each of which will go from each village. They, again, will do exactly the same, and elect a landowner, an occupier, and a labourer to represent them at the county branch. The county branch will do the same thing. And so it works out perfectly simply, and when they arrive in London you will find that the Central Council of the Union is composed one-third of labourers, one-third of occupiers, and one-third of landowners ; and I think that that will be a very fair and proper and equal representation, because they are going to be three partners in the same concern. It is obvious, therefore, that they ought all to be equally represented

Delegates to be Paid.

Of course, you may say to me that it is all very well for me to take railway tickets and go backwards and forwards to meetings, but how are labouring men going to get to those meetings? Well, I say, of course, all delegates will be entitled to receive their out-of-pocket expenses when they are on the business of the Union, and also, in the case of labourers, their day's wages when they are absent from their ordinary work. If that was not to be done it would be a mockery to give you representation, because you could not attend the meetings. The Union will pay the delegates out of its funds for attending meetings on its own business; and it ought to be very glad to do so, because if it did not your voices would not be heard in the councils of the Union.

A Branch in Every Parish.

That is the organisation which I propose to establish, with your consent and by your efforts, and on behalf of yourselves, in every parish in the United Kingdom.

Railway Rates.—What the Union has done.

What will be the result ? Take, for instance, a question like the one that is agitating us so much now all over the country, the question of railway rates. Now how would it enable us to deal with that ? Because you and I, gentlemen, are just like a flock of sheep, and are not organised, and do not know what to do. The railways have seized this opportunity, when we are at our last extremity, to raise their rates all over the kingdom for the carriage of home produce. I am sorry for one reason that they have done it, but from another point of view I am very glad, because it really has roused the country to the truth of what I am saying—that if you choose to lie down in the road, and will not get up to help yourselves, how can you wonder if everybody that goes by gives you a kick and thinks that you deserve it? (Cheers.) Let me point out to you what you have already done towards getting these railway rates reduced by the very threat of combining which I have made on your behalf. I say I am rather glad that the railways have done this. I am glad for this reason : because we shall get the whole interest of the towns with us in this matter. They are just as much interested as we are in home produce not being carried at too high a rate ; and I need not tell you that if the railways of this country are going to fight the towns and the agricultural interest together, there is no doubt whatever which will win in that contest.

But, at the same time, I invite you to consider the practical result that this Agricultural Union has had, even before it is formed. It is a curious thing, but my speech at York on the 5th of this month was the first public speech

in which the railway rates of this country were attacked ; and my speech at
Winchester last Saturday, made on behalf of those whom I wish to join this
Union, that is, the whole of agriculture, was I believe, the next. Now, the
great sinners in this respect that I noticed were the London, Brighton, and
South Coast Railway. I said in my speech at Winchester this : Let the
London, Brighton, and South Coast Railway take care ; for if, when I get to
Tunbridge on the 25th instant, I find that those rates are not altered, I will
tell them something that will make them more careful of their position in the
future. What do I read in the papers this morning ? That the London,
Brighton, and South Coast Railway Company have commenced a reduction of
their new rates. (Cheers).

Well, I say, gentlemen, what is that—and I have said it before ? I am
nothing absolutely myself. You are everything in this matter. I have
spoken on your behalf. It is the National Agricultural Union casting its
shadow before that they fear, when they are retracing their steps and
reducing their rates. (Cheers.) Now, if they did this simply because you
threatened to organise—(A voice: Will the railway companies pay the
agricultural labourers back their money ?)—No, I am afraid we shall not get
anything back in that way from the railway companies. I do not think
that we shall get anything back out of the railway companies, because
when we take a ticket to London, if we do not use it we do not get the
money back.

Now, I have pointed out to you this, and I ask that gentleman there
particularly to attend to this point: if the railway rates are increased on
agricultural produce it must diminish the profits which the person who sends
them gets. If they are reduced it increases those profits. If I make you
absolutely certain that when the profits are increased you get your fair share
of them, every agricultural labourer will get his fair share of anything I can
get off the railway rates. Now, that ought to be as evident, I think, to my
friend there as it is to me. Cannot every agricultural labourer in this room
see this, that if I make an attempt by this Agricultural Union, as I hope we
shall soon do, to get some of the unjust taxes taken off the land, whether
they are rates, whether they are railway rates, or whatever they are, then I
increase the profits of the land ; and if I make you certain, as I do by the
scheme, that you will get your fair share of those profits, then I say that you
are as much interested in it as I am, or anybody else. (Cheers.) I quite
admit that my friend's interruption was excusable, because I have not yet
got to the point where I show you exactly how I do it. Now, if he will give
me his attention for a moment, I am coming to that point next.

The Labourer's Capital.

We have seen that you are going to have an equal representation and an
equal voice on the Council, but how is it that you are going to get your
fair share of the profits ? Well, gentlemen, I look at these matters like
others, as a pure matter of business, and I say that if there are three partners
engaged in working a concern, unless one partner can show that he ought to
have more than another, they ought to be willing to share and share alike in
the profits. There used to be an old saying when I was a boy that a farmer
ought to make three rents, one for himself, one for his labourers, and one
for his landlord. Well, I think that that is a very fair statement of the
case. I think that we ought to divide the profits of the land equally between all the three classes who are engaged in it. (A voice : How about
the labourer's capital ?) My friend says "How about the capital ?" but the
wages that he gets are the interest upon his capital. The labourer's capital
is his strength, his thews and sinews. He gets interest upon them in the
form of wages. The landlord's capital is the money with which he has

bought the lands and called into existence the buildings, drains, and permanent improvements he has put upon it. And now I will tell my friend a thing that may, perhaps, surprise him, because an illustration is worth a pound of argument.

Why the Labourer preferred a Landlord.

In the village of which I was telling you, some of the cottages have always belonged to me, but at one time some of the cow cottages belonged to a man who died. His estate was cut up into lots, and it was going to be offered by auction. The labouring tenants all came to me and said this ; "Are you going to buy these places or not ? because we have got a certain amount of money put by, and we can borrow on the security of our holdings the sum that is necessary to buy them, but if you will buy them would we rather you would buy them than us, and we will not bid against you." Now, why was that ? Not the least, or not entirely, because I was a good landlord.

The reason was this : it was a pure matter of business. They said, "It will cost us £200 to buy our holding. Part of that we shall have to borrow, and part of that we shall pay ourselves. Therefore, £200 will be gone in that way. But if you buy it with your money, we know quite well that you will let us have it at less rent than the interest on the £200 will come to." Everybody who has got £200 is entitled to think how he can invest it best. If you invest money in buying land, it is quite certain that you will not get more than two per cent. If you invest money, as these people wanted to do, and did, in buying stock to work their own land, it was quite certain that at that time at any rate—I do not say now but then—they would get ten or twelve per cent. on their money. Therefore, as men of business, they were quite right in saying, "We would rather that you would put your money at two per cent. in it than put our own." That is an answer to my friend there. That is what the working men did themselves, not as a matter of favour to me, but as a matter of business. They said, "We prefer that your money should lie at two per cent. rather than ours." (Laughter.) And there is nothing very odd about that.

Of course, there are a great many arguments that rest upon that point, but as I do not intend to keep you the whole afternoon, I really cannot go into them ; but I know that you have sense enough as men of business to appreciate that point. I was dealing with—I will not call it the interruption, but the friendly remark of the gentleman in front of me that there was "capital invested." Yes there is. We have all three got capital. The landlord is willing to take two per cent. The tenant wants more because he puts his whole brain and energy into it besides. The labourer's capital is his power and strength to work the land. I say we ought all to get interest on our capital, and I have never found that labourers are less fair or less reasonable than any other class of men when you come to the question of division of profits. But they do say this. (A voice: How much for your services, my lord ?) My friend shall have them. I will not say that they are worth nothing, but he shall have them for nothing. (Cheers.)

A Sliding Scale of Wages.

Now, gentlemen, I want to come to the point which will interest you most in this scheme, and that is, how are we going to secure that you will have your fair share in the profits of anything that you may assist us to obtain ? I say that we are going to take this principle to start with : The three partners are all to have an equal share in the profits. The question is, what is the easiest way to adopt with a view of carrying that into practice ? Well, I say now what I said six years ago at Lincoln, but there were not so many people who thought so then as there are now, that the fairest way would be a sliding scale of wages according to the value of agricultural produce, because then, if agricultural produce goes up, your wages go up, and, if agricultural produce remains where it is, of course we all know that there are very few profits at all to be divided. But what we are talking of now is the better state of things which you and I want to help each other to obtain. What is to be your share of it ? Well, I say, can anybody suggest a better way than a sliding scale of wages, by which wages should rise according to the price of agricultural produce ?

And I can go further, and I can say that for myself—and I believe that I may speak for many others also—I have not the slightest objection to a sliding scale of rents too, if it is practicable. If we are going to discuss this matter, do not let us put it in this way, "Oh, he is a landlord. You know you cannot mention the question of rent to him." Or, "He is a labourer. You must not talk 'about wages." Or, "He is a tenant. We cannot talk about profits." I say that these are the very questions that we want to talk to these very people about. Come to me if you like, and prove to me that I am useless, that I ought to go, that I ought to have no rent; but do not turn your back on me and say, "I will not discuss it with you." Come to me and say that you think so if you do, and I will prove to you that you are wrong, or else you shall convince me that I am wrong; and when you have con-vinced me, I will make my bow, and go and see where I can be of more use than I am here.

But let us discuss these things together, without keeping something back. I am quite willing—I always am—to discuss all these questions—three partners, three interests, three profits all alike, a sliding scale of wages and a sliding scale of rents, if it can be arranged. And then I think that we have solved the whole difficulty if we put this principle into our Agricultural Union. But this I do say, that neither we nor any other body of men could rightly interfere in any case with individual contracts, but we should adopt that principle in our dealings with each other, and if two men could not come to an agreement, there is nothing that I know of to prevent such a Union as this from appointing an Arbitration Committee in every county, or in every town if you like, composed equally of landlords, tenants, and labourers, to discuss and decide these questions when they are brought before them in individual cases. I think that it is better to let men settle things in a friendly way themselves if they will; but it is also well to have in reserve a known principle to which they can appeal, and it is also a great thing as members of one great Union to feel that if you do differ it need not become a question of bad feeling or of losing your respect for one another, but you can say, " I think one thing, you think another. How would it be to ask the Arbitration Committee of our Union to decide the matter ?" That would be a common-sense way of dealing with such questions.

How the Sliding Scale will Work.

Now let me give an instance of exactly how that would work out—the sliding scale of wages. Suppose we take as a round number the price of wheat at 30s. a quarter, and let us say that wages are 2s. a day. This is only an idea of my own. Of course the Union can settle its own terms when it likes, but for want of a better suggestion I will put this before you. This is what I put at Lincoln six years ago. Suppose that wages should rise 3d. a day for every 5s. a quarter that wheat and other corn rose in value. I think that that would be a very fair proportion. What you would get then would be that when you get wheat at 35s. you would get wages at 2s. 3d. When you got to 40s. you would get half a crown. When you got to 45s. you would get 2s. 9d., and when you got to 50s. a quarter you would get wages at 3s. a day. (A Voice : What would be the wages at a 25s. average ?) Well, that, of course, is a matter of very great difficulty, and what we are face to face with is this—and I tell you straight out on this platform—that if things go on much longer as they are, it will not be a question of 2s. a day : it will be a question of no wages at all. (Cheers.) You cannot help it, because, if there is no money to pay a thing out of, with the best will in the world nobody can pay it. That is what it really comes to, and that is what makes me stand here and tell you that you are on the brink of a precipice of which you little know the depth, and when you turn from the edge of it, as by the help of Providence I hope you will, you will not know what you have escaped ; but the point upon which that gentleman has put his finger is well worthy of your attention, viz.: What will happen if produce goes down and down ?—and you and I must unite together in this National Agricultural Union to take such measures as will prevent this and bring back prosperity to Agriculture. (Cheers.) If we do that we shall all have our share in the profits and in the rise. If we leave it alone and do nothing, I am perfectly certain, not only that rents will cease to be paid altogether, but that tenants' profits will cease altogether ; and as to wages, I will ask you as sensible men, in that case where are wages to come from at all ? There are thousands of acres in this country which any one of you might go and occupy and till for the asking, without paying any rent whatever at all. Why do not you go and do it ? Simply because you know that at present prices you could not make it pay. (Cheers.)

A Fair Critic.

I had a letter before I came into this room from a gentleman that many of you, I believe, are acquainted with, although he is not personally known to myself—Mr. Joseph Robinson .Now, I take a man as I find him always, and I am entitled to judge him by that letter. It was a fair letter. It was a straightforward letter. It was the letter of a man who was not thinking of himself, but who was thinking, "What will be the effect of this upon the labourer ?" He said, "When a hundred acres make £600 I do not think we get our fair share." Gentlemen, I will put one fact before you. I am a farmer myself. I grow a hundred acres of wheat every year. This year I sold my hundred acres of wheat, not for £600, not for £500, not for £400, and not for £300, but for £260. Gentlemen, it cost me £400 out of pocket to grow that hundred acres of wheat ; and, I ask you, can you imagine a state of things more dangerous to the labourers of this country than that all this land which now grows wheat shall go out of cultivation ? You cannot, believe me, cultivate these large tracts of bad land without the aid of capital. You cannot do it. It pays you that they should be cultivated, because every acre of cultivated land employs four labourers, and if corn is to cease to be grown, as cease it will, if it will not pay, because nobody can go on paying £400 out of one hand, and receiving only £260 in the other. I say that that constitutes the danger and difficulty of the crisis.

But now suppose that you had this sliding scale of wages, and suppose that—not taking that gloomy view which my friend does, and which this Union is exactly the very thing and the only thing which will enable us to prevent—you assist us in going in for more prosperity, see, I beseech you, how that would affect a very simple question. Now when I talk of the price of wheat being raised to 50s. a quarter, there are many ways in which that could be done. If we had better trade in this country to-morrow, if freights were to rise, and if people were to charge more for bringing us wheat across the sea, if we were to have a war, if we were to have a hundred things, we might have wheat at 50s. a quarter to-morrow. We had it at 40s. a quarter last year. It is not so many years ago since I sold wheat at 60s. a quarter. We might have it at that for a hundred reasons. I will ask you this simple question : Would you be better off with wheat at 50s. a quarter and wages at 3s. a day, than you are with it now at 30s. a quarter, and lower still, and wages at 2s. ? I can prove absolutely that you would. Take the difference between the wages at 3s. and 2s. One is 12s. a week, and the other is 18s. That is 6s. a week difference in wages. (A voice : How about the men in the towns ?) I am talking about the agriculturists. I am quite able to talk to the people in the towns. (Laughter and cheers.) Let me tell my friend at this moment, and that is all that I shall say to him, that the towns are heartily with us in this movement, and they told me so at York. "Come," they said, "to Birmingham, and you will be surprised at the reception you will get. We are beginning to find out now that agriculture and trade are sister industries "—(cheers)—"and we are determined that agriculture, being a sister industry, shall have fair play, and we are determined that the British farmer shall have his chance of putting his produce on the market." That is my present reply to the gentleman who has asked, "How about the towns ?"

I beg that he will not draw our attention off the point, because it is an important one—the wages of agricultural labourers if they come into this scheme. I take the worst case of all, which is wheat, because, suppose barley were to go up, or oats were to go up, you would have nothing to add to your bread bill, because we eat neither barley nor oats. Now, suppose there should be a rise in wheat, and it was to go up to 50s. a quarter, I was showing you, when my friend interrupted me, that you would get 6s. a week extra. Now, what would you lose on your bread bill ? Suppose that you had got a very large family—and, gentlemen, correct me if I am wrong—you perhaps would buy fifteen loaves a week, or something like that. Fifteen loaves, at the present price of 4½d., will come to 5s. 7½d. Supposing that bread went up to 6d. a loaf instead of 4½d.—and remember that that is a great supposition, because I showed at York, from the profit that the bread companies are making now, which is something like 30 per cent., bread ought not to rise, and that even if wheat were at 50s. a quarter, bread ought to be at something like its present price, and if you will join me in co-operation, we can get it down to its just price and keep it. (Cheers.) But I am taking the worst case against myself, and I say, supposing that bread rose to 6d. a loaf. Sixpence a loaf for fifteen loaves is half as many shillings, that is, 7s. 6d. If you take the old price of bread, 5s. 7½d., you will get 1s. 10½d. addition to your bread bill. Now, of course, you have to take that off your 6s. a week extra wages ; but what is the result ? Supposing that trade were to revive to morrow, and wheat were to go up to 50s. a quarter, and you had this arrangement that I proposed to you, you would make a net gain of the difference between 1s. 10d. a week and 6s. a week, and you would have 4s. 2d. clear in your pocket. Well, now, I say that it is worth your while, as business men, to consider that special view.

The Tea Duty.

But I will take another and more favourable one now. I have taken one against myself. I will take one in favour of myself. We are not here dealing with any question of a new duty, but I say at the present moment we have duties on certain things. How about the tea duty? We put a duty upon tea which comes out of the consumer's pocket, but it is no use to you or to me. There is nobody in England that can grow an acre of tea if he tries. Therefore all the money that we have to pay for the tea duty is undoubtedly taken out of the consumer's pocket, and it puts nothing in yours or mine, and if we are going to have a duty—of course the revenue must be raised—why in the name of common sense cannot we put it upon something that we do grow in this country? Why not take it off tea and put it on the foreign fruit and vegetables, for you grow these upon your allotment ? It would not cost the consumer any more, because he pays a duty now on the tea, and tea is not a luxury. It is quite as much a necessary for poor people as their daily bread. Why not take the duty off tea and put it on something which you and I do grow ? [A voice: Barley.] Well barley is usually associated with a different drink to tea. (Laughter.) I was coming to that presently. [A voice: Foreign barley.] I will take the foreign barley that my friend has mentioned.

The Beer Duty.

It grieves me to the soul as a Free Trader to think that we pay the duty on beer that we do. We have a duty of 6s. 3d. on every barrel of beer consumed in this country. That, just like the tea duty, does not benefit a single producer in this country. If you want 6s. 3d. a barrel of beer for duty for the purpose of revenue, why in the world cannot you put it on in such a way as to secure that beer should be brewed from English barley and hops ? (Loud cheers.) If you did that I am quite certain the consumer would not lose anything, because he pays the duty now; and I am quite certain that you and I would gain a great deal, because we should get 10s. a quarter more for our barley, whether it is grown on a field or on an allotment. And I am certain of this, too—that many a fellow who likes a glass of good beer—and I like one myself—(hear, hear)—would be able to get one which would be less likely to disagree with him than what he gets now (Hear, hear.)

Now, gentlemen, I simply propose to you as business men, and you will see perfectly well that there are many of these questions which, if we were to meet together and discuss them, as you and I are discussing them now, we should find are not in the least difficult questions. There is no difficulty about them at all except this. This is the difficulty : when three men will keep their backs turned to each other they cannot expect to see very much of each other. (Cheers.) If you and I, instead of keeping our backs turned to each other, will turn round, all three classes face to face, and discuss them like man and man, I assure you you do not know how many things can be done, and done without delay, and done in such a way that the whole country would be delighted that they should be done in order to assist us. And I ask you to take home with you that one question, if you like, of the beer duty, and ask yourselves whether the thing does not work out as I say in that case ; whether we might not take the duty off what it is on now, and put it in such a way that you could make beer of English materials, and, if so, whether that would not raise the price of barley ; and if so, whether, under my arrangement, it would not raise your wages too, and raise them in such a way that you would not have to take anything off them for the price of bread. I think that that is a point which is well worthy of your considering. (A Voice: A foreign flour tax.) Oh, I did not dare mention that, you know. (Laughter.) I must inform my friend that that is a sacred subject. I dare not talk about that. Oh no, we must not do that, because to do that might raise the price of bread, and even if you were to get 10s. a week wages more we must not raise the price of bread. Let that gentleman turn at once to the contemplation of English beer, and do not let him think any more about flour. (Laughter.)

Chambers of Agriculture.

I desire, if I may now, to say a word on a matter of business which is an important one if we are going to found this Union, as I hope we may ; and that is that there are in the country, as you know, certain organisations which are called Chambers of Agriculture and Farmers' Clubs. I have been endeavouring in every way—and successfully so far—to work in harmony with them, because I think that when you want to carry a great movement you ought to carry everybody with you, and more particularly those who have shown in the past that they are willing to stir and move in the right direction. The Organising Committee of the Conference made a report the other day in which they adopted my proposals. That was all right and we were both parties to that. But then the next day in the papers somebody put in, twenty-four hours before this report could be circulated, a statement exactly the reverse of the truth, viz., that there had been a meeting and that my scheme had been given up. Now, as exactly the contrary was the case, and my scheme was adopted, I think that it is very important this should be known, because I have had letters since from people who say, " I am very sorry to hear that your scheme is given up, because anything like the Chambers of Agriculture as at present constituted is not at all what we want." I want to define my position exactly in this matter, because it is best for us all.

Now the report proposed, and I consented that the Central Chamber of Agriculture, when they met at the end of this month, should appoint a Committee to confer with me, they on one side, and I on the other, as to the rules of this new Union. Now this is what will happen. The Chambers of Agriculture of course represent—and are quite right to do it—the fourteen thousand members who belong to them; but I in this matter, as the author of the scheme, have a responsibility, and a great one, before the 240,000 tenant farmers who do not belong to them, and before the 2,000,000 labourers who do not belong to them either. And I say this, if the Committee can suggest any improvements I shall respectfully consider them, and of course adopt them, but I will not be a party to watering down this scheme so as to make it anything like what the Chambers of Agriculture are now.

I must take my stand, and I shall do so without moving a single hair's breadth, on these great principles—representative principles, partnership principles, which I have laid down, and I will tell you an excellent reason why I must do so. In a public document for which I made myself responsible I told the labourers this, "I will undertake that if you join the Union you shall have your full share and voice in the control of it." Gentlemen, I will undertake that as long as I have anything to do with it; but if any scheme is proposed in which that or any other principle which I have laid down does not find a place, I say at once that I will have nothing to with it, because I have given a promise and am bound to make my words good. I say that, not because I believe that there is the slightest misunderstanding between myself and the Chambers of Agriculture, but because, as I point out, I must take the personal responsibility before the people of this country as the author of the scheme, and I am bound not to lend my name to it a moment longer than I think it is going to be conducted on those principles of which alone I approve, and which I have laid down and bound myself to in this letter which I wrote to the labourers of England. (Cheers.)

Now, gentlemen, what is true is this—and I ask you to recognise it frankly with me—the Chambers of Agriculture contain many admirable men. We cannot afford to lose them, and therefore it is that the moment they are satisfied that this new organisation will cover their ground and something more, I hope that they will see their way to set free their members to take that part in the new organisation, to which nobody will welcome them more gladly than myself. I did undertake—and with your help I will do it—to unite agriculturists.

We must have a new organisation, gentlemen, because, however good the old one may once have been, if it has existed for twenty-five years without filling the gap, and without coming to the front in this great crisis, it is quite certain that if you and I are to move forward in the right direction, we must have something conducted on new and representative principles Then I

D

believe that, if we get that, we shall get all the best men out of the old organisations; in fact, all the men who like to come in, including the vast body of agriculturists who have hitherto held aloof because they have never been able to see the use of joining associations which, however good, really confine themselves principally to discussion. I want myself that we should talk exactly as much as necessary to bring ourselves to one mind on the question—that we should not stop there, but act, and act at once, as we must if we are to save the great industry by which we live.

Programme of the Union.

Now, gentlemen, I have a few words more, and of course I cannot trespass any further upon your great indulgence, but I have been asked, "If you mean this Union to attract us, why do you not make your programme a bigger one?" Let me remind you of this. The moment you adopt this resolution, which I trust you will, as unanimously as it was done at York and in the South of England, the Union is your Union and not mine. I have no right to fetter you or tie you beforehand to any programme which I do not know that you are unanimous upon. It is for you, after you form the Union, to put upon the programme anything which you wish to be carried out, and you can do it by your own votes, expressed constitutionally by the machinery which I have placed at your disposal. I have put upon the programme one or two things of the greatest importance, such as reducing local burdens upon land and co-operation, and the labourers will see at once that, inasmuch as they are going to share all the profits, it is as much to their interest as anybody else's that we should do it. But do remember this, gentlemen.

The idea of the Union may be an excellent one, and I believe is, and I, no doubt, have the happiness to be the author of it; but, when we remember that no living statesman hardly, and very few dead ones, have ever suggested a remedy for agriculture without at once falling through the ice up to their necks, and being rescued with considerable difficulty, it is a little hard to call upon me at a moment's notice to bring into existence a full-blown programme of which everybody will approve. (Cheers.) I have not the presumption to attempt anything of the kind. What I want to do is to convince you of this, first of all, that I am perfectly sincere in desiring to present you an instrument for working out your own salvation—(cheers)—and, secondly, that in that I do not desire in the least to favour one class more than another. And I want to go a little deeper—I want to bring people a little more into harmony, a little more face to face, and to do away with a few of those bad feelings which so often embitter our country life' which we all regret, and which we do not like quite to take the first step to put an end to. If we can only do that we shall have done a great thing.

And thirdly, I have pointed out that in my own uneventful life, I have given you at any rate some proof of my desire to be of service to you when you had no votes at all. Further, that I now propose to give you a machinery which will safeguard you on your own Council, and give you a share of any profits there may be.

With regard to the programme, I do not assume to myself the right to put upon it anything upon which you are not agreed. However, from to-day two further objects will take their place upon it. One is a recognition of the principle that the three classes engaged in agriculture are three partners entitled equally to divide the profits, whether that result can be best arrived at by a sliding scale of wages and rents, or by some other machinery which the Union may think better adapted to give effect to that principle; another is the reduction of unfair railway rates on home produce.

Now let me pay a compliment, if I may, to the Great Eastern Railway Company in this matter, because we must be fair all round to everybody. I believe they have not increased their rates upon agricultural produce. One of their directors assured me that they had not. (A Voice : "Oh yes, they have," and laughter.) Well, sir, I am very sorry that it is so, but really I had hoped that I might pay them a deserved compliment by way of exception ; but since my friend says that it is not so, I am afraid I must include them with other railways, but not, I hope, to the same extent. I say we will place upon our programme from this moment the reduction of unfair railway rates upon home produce ; in that we shall have the support of the towns equally with the country, and if you wish to carry a great public movement, I need not tell you how enormously important it is that the towns should be with you. In this country they are the centres of our great industries, and they can help us, if they will, to bring our project to a successful issue.

A Fairy Gift.

I believe that I have made the situation perfectly clear. I leave it with the greatest confidence in your hands. This new Agricultural Union I want to make a New Year's gift to the labourers of England. It is their own. They can manage it, in concert with the other classes, after it is formed, as they will ; but let them remember that I have refrained from writing upon the programme anything likely to divide or anything which would strike at the root of that principle which 1 have laid down for the guidance of the Union. Remember, therefore, if I may put it so, that it is a fairy gift which will only be useful to you, and only be blessed to you, if you use it for the great purpose for which it is given to you. It will only be useful if you make it, as I hope and trust you will, not only a great Agricultural Union of interests, but, in the truest and deepest possible sense, a union of hearts. (Cheers.)

SPEECH

BY THE

EARL OF WINCHILSEA & NOTTINGHAM,

*Delivered at a Meeting of Agriculturists, held in the Guildhall,
Plymouth, on Thursday, January 19th, 1893.*

LORD CLINTON IN THE CHAIR.

THE EARL OF WINCHILSEA AND NOTTINGHAM : My Lords, Ladies and Gentlemen, your Chairman has been kind enough to guarantee to me on your behalf a kind and indulgent hearing. But I am still more glad to hear from him that he can guarantee me a general acquiescence in those principles which I come here to lay before you, because more than that I neither aspire to nor desire. I am very glad indeed to accept your invitation to come to Plymouth, because I remember that many years ago, when I was at a more impressionable age, I came down to the West Country to spend a happy vacation. I went to Cornwall, and I left it with the impression, which still remains upon me, that I had never seen so many pretty women before in all the course of my life. (Laughter and cheers, and a voice : I admire your taste, Sir.) Plymouth is very near to Cornwall, and in the absence of ladies from this meeting, which I deplore, but whose blushes on this account I am the more able to save, I may say that nothing which I have seen since I arrived at Plymouth has weakened, everything has rather strengthened and confirmed, my first impression of the ladies of the West of England. (Laughter.)

The Wheal Owls Disaster.

May I, in passing, take this, the first, public opportunity I have had of conveying a personal tribute of sympathy to the town of St. Just in the great bereavement that has fallen upon it. If the people of St. Just have forgotten me, I have not forgotten them, nor have I forgotten that in more than one family there I received a kind and hospitable welcome when I went down to Cornwall. Therefore I thought that it would not be impertinent on my part if, the first time my attention was drawn to this great disaster, I wrote straight to the Chairman of the Relief Committee, to express my heartfelt sympathy, and to contribute my mite towards the relief of those who are suffering. I trust that it may be found possible to succeed in the efforts which are being made to rescue the bodies of those who have fallen, from their present position; but if not, and if no formal consecration service can take place, I hope that ministers of all denominations will assure their flocks that the spot on which a brave man falls in the discharge of his duty, whether it be on the sea or on the battle-field, on the land or in the mine, is as sacred from that moment as the blessing of priest or layman can make it. (Cheers.)

Town and Country.

Is it not a curious fact that when I come down here to speak to you of unity, and the union which ought to prevail between all classes connected with agriculture, before I can get to my topic I find that I am arrested on the threshold by a wider sympathy still, and that we are compelled, in passing, to offer a sincere tribute to an industry to which we do not belong? And what does that mean? Why it means this—not only that the interests of all classes engaged in agriculture are one, but that all our interests are one. And therefore I rejoice when I come to a large and important town, such as that in which I find myself to-day, to be able to point the moral to which your Chairman has alluded, that in this matter we seek no selfish gain, we have no selfish object in view, and that to rescue agriculture, if it may be, from the deplorable state in which at the present moment it is, is a matter of national concern, and one which interests you in this town no less in your corporate capacity—yes, and from the point of view of your individual incomes—than it concerns those who are more strictly engaged in agriculture. (Cheers.)

Overtaken by the Tide.

Gentlemen, has this crisis been exaggerated or not? Here in the West of England I am happy to think that, although you are passing through troubled waters, still you have not, I believe, felt the full stress of the weather under which we in the East and North-east and South-east of England are labouring. May I assure you, from my own personal knowledge, that in those parts of England there are many landlords who are receiving no rents at all, many tenants who are making no profits, yes, many labourers who are getting no wages. There are thousands of acres which, up to the present time, have been growing corn for the sustenance of the people, now out of cultivation, and pleading for something to be devised which will bring them back their usefulness, and occupy the labouring class upon them. That is no exaggerated statement; it can be maintained by statistics. And, now, what do I say to you here? If you are not in that terrible position yourselves, remember this: If we are overtaken by the tide together, shall I say to you that, because I stand on a somewhat higher rock, I will not come to your help before the tide overwhelms you? How do we know how high this tide is going to rise? It is our turn to-day, but it may be yours to-morrow. Therefore, even from a selfish point of view, you cannot stand aloof from those who are engaged in the same occupation as yourselves in other parts of England, and who ask you, before it is too late, to join with them, if possible, in saving the great industry by which they live. (Cheers.)

The West to go " Solid."

I come to you with an encouraging message from the North, from the South, and from the East of England. At York, where twelve counties were represented; at Winchester, where four counties were represented; at Ipswich, where four counties not only represented, but where, by special invitation, the labourers were asked to attend—yes, and did attend, and walked through eight inches of snow to be present—I say that from all those places I bring you a unanimous vote in support of the principle which your Chairman has said that you, too, are willing to endorse. And so, if I may use a word which (if I remember my last visit aright) is rather peculiar to yourselves, I ask that the West of England will do as the North, the South, and the East have done, and that it will go "solid" for the National Agricultural Union. (Cheers.)

Competition.

Now, if we require any arguments to convince us that some such organisation is necessary, they will be found, I think, in a review of the present state of agriculture. What has led us into the terrible position in which we are? Partly natural causes and partly artificial ones. I do not ask you to remove the natural causes, but I do say that we may do something to remove the artificial ones. (Cheers.) It is perfectly true that our condition is caused very greatly by the fall of prices which comes from foreign competition. Nobody who has studied the question can deny this ; but that I hold to be a natural cause. It is a cause of which, if you look widely over the world, you cannot find it in your heart to complain, because it means that as the ages go on the produce of each country finds more and more a market in different places from that in which it was produced, to the benefit both of those who grow it and of those who eventually consume it. But, gentlemen, what I desire to point out to you is that these natural causes have been brought upon us with crushing effect, because they have been stimulated by artificial causes within our own control, which we ought to remove.

Disorganisation.

Now, I say that competition coming upon us as it has, and finding us in a disorganised state, has been able to take an advantage of the home producer which it never would have been able to take had he been organised, and I shall give you one or two examples.

The New Railway Rates.

First of all, there is a question which is uppermost, I think, in our minds at this moment—the question of railway rates. (Loud cheers.) Would the railways have ever dealt with an organised interest of our importance in the way that they are dealing now with you and with me ? And in this matter, gentlemen, let it not be supposed that I am attacking the interests of the railways. On the contrary, I say that by the policy which they are pursuing they are mistaking their real interests altogether. (Cheers.) The foreign producer may take to himself wings, the white wings of his ships, and may fly away from our railways altogether. But you and I, gentlemen, are among their permanent customers. It must be among the home producers that the railways ought to look for their permanent clients ; and therefore, when they are putting upon an industry already depressed a burden too grievous to be borne, those who point this out to them, and point it out in time, are not only serving the best interests of agriculture, but the best interests of the railway companies themselves. (Loud cheers.)

Now, gentlemen, whenever I come to any particular locality I think it respectful to address myself, during part of the time which I am privileged to speak, to any local comments which may have been made upon the scheme. But, in the first place, before I do so let me read to you, in simple proof of the point of view that I have just noticed, part of a letter which is signed by a Liskeard Tradesman ; and Liskeard is not very far, as you know, from Plymouth. He says this, " The goods charged at the higher rates are conveyed in the same trucks with those at the lower, and their handling is no more troublesome or risky. Yet without any apparent reason "—yes, that is why we hate it, gentlemen ; there is no reason for what they are doing at the present moment—" without any appparent reason the railway companies are allowed to name this article to pay 50, 100, or 200 per cent. more than identical other articles conveyed next to it." And he goes on to point out that the rises in rates in the articles which he names are something like 60 or 70 per cent. upon the old rates. We are told by the railway companies, "Oh, you have no idea how complicated this question is. Lots of our managers have been taken from their duties ; lots of our clerks are working day and night making out new rates." Gentlemen, let me put it thus. The thing is not complicated at all. What they can very easily 'do is this—and we shall be perfectly satisfied with it—whenever there is an old rate and a new rate let them take the lowest. (Laughter and cheers.)

A Personal Question.

I have been honoured with a further communication in the public press of Plymouth this morning. I spare the writer any quotation from it, except from the last sentence, but inasmuch as he writes from the Trade Union Hall in Plymouth, and may be supposed, therefore, to assume some authority (I hope without any ground) on behalf of those whose hall he writes from, I desire to point out that, in assuming the position of a champion of the railway companies—which really the letter does, because you cannot run with the hare and hunt with the hounds—he is not, I think, taking the course which will commend itself even to those whom he assumes to represent. He asks me a personal question at the end of his letter, and this I freely admit, that when anyone assumes the position which I occupy to day, and invites his countrymen to consider a great possible remedy for a great national evil, everyone has the right to look as closely as possible into his public, ay! and into his private career. Gentlemen, I do not shrink from any such ordeal. I court it. (Cheers.) Therefore, when the writer asks me this question, "Lord Winchilsea himself, as he is lord of a manor, will he please inform us, if this landlords' union is formed"—gentlemen, 17,000 agricultural labourers accepted it unanimously yesterday at Ipswich by the mouth of their representatives—"if this landlords' union is formed, what he and his colleagues are going to do with the many acres of the people's common rights that they, by the 3600 or 3700"—it is well to be accurate—"separate measures of land laws, have got upon the Statute Book for the relief of the poor." Well, gentlemen, I say that if we have been so fortunate—though I was not aware of it—as to get 3600 separate measures of land laws to place those acres upon the Statute Book for the relief of the poor, by bringing them, I suppose, into cultivation, by making a country worth nothing worth something, and employing labourers where they were employing nobody, I say that we have established a claim which I had no idea we had to the gratitude of this country. (Laughter and cheers.)

A Lord of the Manor.

What the National Agricultural Union may do I cannot tell you, as I am not privileged to speak for them. They will soon be in existence, and will speak for themselves. I can only inform the writer what I have done in the case of my own land, as he refers to me as the lord of a manor. Gentlemen, I and my ancestors—for an ancestor of my own in 1798, nearly 100 years ago, gave evidence before a Royal Commission to that effect—have taken these lands which were worth nothing, because they were growing nothing but furze and rabbits, and, by putting our money into them, we have turned them into good pasture, and we have let that good pasture at reasonable rents to small tenants. (Cheers.) I will go further. I think that a lord of the manor who has done that may consider himself no bad trustee for the public good. But it is generally supposed that a man's duties to the labourers and to other people are confined to his own estate, or at any rate to his own manor; but a case has occurred on my own property to which I direct the attention of the writer of the letter.

Allotments.

There is a village in Northamptonshire—I will give him the name : it is Corby, not far from Kettering—where I do not own an acre of land, and where I am not lord of the manor at all ; but the working men of that parish came to me and they said, "We cannot obtain on our own manor land suitable for allotments. Will you give us a grass field which is next to our parish for that purpose ?" Well, 1 asked my tenant, who views these things in the same light as I do, and he gave the field up. I gave it to these men, thirty or forty of them, for allotments, and at the very moment at which I am speaking to you, if I am not mistaken—at any rate the order has been given—men employed by my money are engaged in draining this very land for the use of the allotment holders upon it. (Cheers.) What other people may do with their land I know not, and I am not responsible. (A voice: "Number one.") Yes, Sir, I take care of number one, like everybody else. (Laughter and cheers.) I admit that in doing this I am taking care of number one; and if you can prove to landlords all over the country that by establishing allotments and small holdings they will be taking care of number one they will do it; and that is what I want to prove to them. My ancestor of 100 years ago, to whom I have alluded already, said this before the Royal Commission: "I have ninety such tenants on my estate at Rutland, and they are the best tenants that I have got. They are doing well, and they are paying their rent." That is what I call taking care of number one, but it is also taking care in the best way that we can of the labourers who are solemnly committed to our charge. (Loud cheers.)

Now, Sir, I will take leave of the writer of that letter. I am much obliged to him for enabling me to place these facts before you; but this I will say in taking leave of him, that I think it my duty not to indicate what other people are to do with their land, but to manage my own business, and to manage it well; and if certain other people were to take that view they would not place themselves in the ridiculous positions that they often occupy. (Cheers.)

Organise.

But now, to pass away, as I am anxious to do, from this personal matter, and to get back to the great question which we are discussing. I have shown you, I think, that competition has much to do with it, and disorganisation has more; and I have given you a great instance of this in the present railway rates, which, as an unorganised interest contending with an organised one, we are not able really to cope with. The question is, "What is to be the remedy for this?" Well, various remedies—conflicting ones, generally—have been proposed. They have been accepted with fervour by one party, and rejected with equal fervour by another. It does not require much arithmetic to show that, even if you have got a million on one side, still if you have got a million on the other, and take one from the other, nothing whatever of a practical nature is left. One person is going to propose a remedy, another equally powerful opposes it on the ground that his own is better. While this is so, you will get nothing from this country, you will get nothing from Parliament, and you will rightly fail, because Parliament has so much business to do that it will not take up any cause unless it is satisfied that those who advocate it know what they mean, and have agreed among themselves beforehand. (Cheers.) Therefore I say that, whatever may be the eventual remedy or remedies to be applied, whether by legislation or otherwise, the first thing that is absolutely certain is this, that unless we organise, as every other great industry has organised, we shall not get it.

Get back the Profits.

Now, what do I propose? I propose this. The scheme which I am about to propound to you rests on those great principles to which your Chairman has alluded. I point out that the interests of all three classes engaged in the land are so much one that the small points on which they differ may fairly be left out of the question. They may differ eventually about the division of profits. That, gentlemen, at the present moment is so small a question as to disappear, because profits have vanished altogether, and therefore we need not talk of dividing them. The question is, How are we going to get back those profits to the land, out of which alone any of the three classes—I do not care which it is—can get either rent, profits, or wages? That is the great question which lies before us, and our interests are absolutely identical in the solution of it.

An Old Adage Revived.

Well, I have got a step farther than this ; and I find that in this matter
it is necessary to advance by somewhat slow degrees. People are not
always prepared to receive a whole project at once. It is better, therefore,
to place the elementary principles first before the country, and when they
are agreed' to, point out something more. And so we get up step by step to
the elevation on which, at last, we want to stand. I have pointed out that,
if all classes are equally interested in returning the profit to the land, it
follows that we are three partners, and entitled to bear equally and to divide
equally the losses and profits of our joint concern. That really is a principle
which has never before been admitted in so many words, and that is one
reason which keeps us asunder. But I can remember that when I was
a boy there was an old saying, which I did not quite understand then, but
which I see now embodies a very valuable truth, and that is, that a farmer
ought to make three profits out of the land, one for himself, one for his
labourers, and one for his landlord. Well, what is that except the recognition
of the very principle which I am laying down, that all three classes are
partners, and entitled equally to divide the losses or profits of their under-
taking ? (Cheers.)

Sliding Scale of Wages.

But, I am asked, how are we going to bring that to a practical form ? I
answer, in this way, unless the Union when it is formed can suggest any
other. What I suggest is that, in order that the labourer may have his share
of any profits which he may assist, by joining this Union, to bring back to
agriculture, he should be entitled—and we should register that, as it were, in
our deed of partnership—to a sliding scale of wages, according to the price of
agricultural produce. Now, that is a point which is not a new one. (Interruption.) Some gentlemen, I think, seem rather disturbed by that proposal.
I do not know why. It is not a new one. It is one which I supported myself
six years ago at Lincoln ; but, remember, it is one which can never be carried
into practical effect unless by a great National Union, composed of all three
classes, agreeing to that principle ; and then, and then only, will the labourer
have the security that he wants, that he will get his share in any rise which
he may join to assist you in gaining.

The Labourer's Guarantee.

Gentlemen, do not forget this, because even I am old enough to remember
it—that when the last rise of prices took place in this country the labourer
did not get his proper share of it. We had wheat at a very high price
compared to what it is now, and yet wages were, if not as low as they are
now, in many parts of the country, I fear, very little higher. Therefore, the
labourer, remembering what happened ten years ago, naturally stands aloof,
and he says, " Yes, prosperity for agriculture may mean prosperity for you,
but not for me; and, if it is to mean prosperity for me, give me some
security : give me some guarantee that I shall join in these profits, and then
I will go with you heart and soul." (Cheers.) Gentlemen, I say that you
ought to give him such a guarantee. I say that he is entitled to such a
guarantee. I say that his labour and his strength are equally essential to
the cultivation of the soil with your capital; that we cannot leave him out
of account; that we have no right to do so; that he is well within his right,
as a matter of justice and equity, in asking to be admitted as an equal
partner into the concern. (Cheers.) Now, gentlemen, when I say that we
adopt this principle, of course I do not mean that in individual cases we are
going to constitute ourselves a "Holy Inquisition," as it were, to ask what
are the arrangements between man and man. But what I say is this, that if

we all go into this Union laying down that principle to start with, then people can make their own bargains with each other fairly upon that principle; and, if they differ, I know not why they should not, as common members of the same Union, refer their dispute, if there be one, or refer their honest difference of view before it becomes a dispute, to a committee composed of an equal number of landlords, occupiers, and labourers, belonging to the National Agricultural Union. (Cheers.)

Separate Unions Condemned.

Now, before I give you exactly what the scheme is, I should like to point out to you that nothing less than this will suffice. No separate organisations, however good, will meet the point. Let me take, first of all, the point of view of landlords. Among these there is no question whatever of any separate organisation. That has not even been mooted. I may pass on to the tenant farmers' point of view. I perfectly admit that the tenant farmers of this country, if they are to act, as they must, as the invaluable intermediaries between the other two classes for extracting the food from the soil, must have a free hand. They must have security for the capital that they put into the land. Yes, they must have more than that. They must have a great deal more than that. They must have, as I put it at York, free access personally to their own landlords. (Cheers.) They must be able to do what every tenant on my property has long known that he can do with regard to me. If he has a suggestion to make by which he can get more out of the land—a suggestion which one business man may make to another— let him come, not through a third party, but by himself, and let him make it. (Prolonged cheers.) And I tell you, gentlemen, that no one ought to watch the result of that experiment with more interest than the landlord. Why, I get many a wrinkle on my own farm from good tenants on the estate. As soon as a tenant comes to me and says,—" I should like to adopt this or that system on my own farm," I say,—" Well, if you would like to, by all means do it. You know more about it than I do. Probably, if I were to adopt it, I might fail, but if I see how you do it first I may very likely succeed." And therefore we have what we want in this matter; we have the best modern improvements constantly applied, by the goodwill both of landlord and tenant, to the cultivation of the soil. And, gentlemen, where you have done that you have done much to remove not only the natural obstacles to success, but those barriers which, above all, I want to break down—artificial barriers between man and man.

A Tenant Farmers' Party.

But I do not think—and I respectfully say so to tenant farmers—that any separate organisation, apart from the other two classes, will really meet this great question as far as the tenant farmers themselves are concerned. I have seen such organisations proposed ; I have seen different programmes sketched out, some of them very inviting, some of them good, some of them bad ; but I notice always that they are to be carried out by "a compact body" of members representing tenant farmers in the House of Commons. I have pointed out before—I say it in no spirit of hostility—but I do on my responsibility point it out here to the tenant farmers of England again—that they cannot, as political matters are now arranged, return a single member in a single constituency of this kingdom without the help of the other two classes connected with the land. Therefore, it is idle to talk of a compact body of members simply to represent the tenant farmer class, because if they decline to join in a great National Agricultural Union, to which they are invited by the two other classes connected with the land—I will not say, " What view will the landlord class take ?"—because we may be able to understand you ;

but what view can the labourers take except this, that you think that your interests are different from their own, and, therefore, when the time comes to choose a representative, they will say, and will rightly say, that, as you have separated yourselves from them in this matter, so they will separate themselves from you in the choice of a representative in Parliament. (Cheers.) Now, gentlemen, I say this, not because I desire for a moment to separate the interests of the three classes, but because I am certain that nothing less than the National Agricultural Union will really obtain for any one of these classes the benefit which it wants.

A Labourers' Union Exposed.

Now, let us take the labourers, for instance. In the East of England—I do not know what it may have been here—some years ago they had a Union of their own, and the object was to raise wages by a sliding scale, very much like the one which I now propose. But not only was the organisation avowedly apart from the tenant farmers and the landlords, but there were no pains taken to conceal the fact that it was against them. It was a question of who was the strongest. That Union was engineered and officered by men who may have been honest and may have meant well, but who were totally misinformed as to those economic conditions which are stronger either than you, or me, or them. The labourers had to pay twopence a week into that Union, and it was supposed to include a sick club as well. Those who knew the actuarial figures told them, to begin with, " The thing is certain to fail. You cannot get out of it the benefits which are promised to you." For a few months wages were increased by the action of that Union, but afterwards they went down lower than they were before, and many poor fellows, who had put their money in on the faith of receiving it back in the form of sick pay, lost every farthing that they had put into that Union. I say, in no spirit of hostility to the people who organised that Union, would it not have been better to organise a Union in which, by the consent, instead of against the will, of the other two classes, you could have got a rise of wages? Would it not have been better to ask someone who knew, whether you really could give the labourers the sick pay which you promised them?

It is possible, as I say, that these separate unions of labourers might have been honestly organised, but they have failed hitherto, and they will always fail, because those who organise them are not well acquainted with the economic conditions which they must fulfil. At any rate, they are a thousand times more likely to succeed when we offer them what I do at this moment, entrance to a Union where they are to be joined to and not separated from the other two classes, where they are to share and share alike with us in the profits of any rise, where they are to have their own representatives upon the Council, and where they are for the first time to be recognised as what they really are—equal partners with ourselves in the great business which we are carrying on. (Cheers.)

The Scheme.

The scheme itself is probably well known to you all. It is that we should establish a great Agricultural Union, membership of which is to be open to all classes connected with the land. We have a different scale of subscriptions, so that those who have the greatest stake may pay the most ; and that, I think, is a very important point, and quite a right one. Also we secure that all three classes should have an equal representation. We are going to have a branch in every parish or group of parishes in England. Also we are going to have district branches in the market town, county branches in the county towns, and, finally, a Council in London representative of the whole ; and, from head to foot of that organisation, on every Council in it, on every committee in it, you will find equally représented in equal numbers the owner, the occupier, and the labourer.

A Fair Offer.

No fairer plan, as far as I know, could possibly be devised than this. I heard a very remarkable statement—and, so far as I know, it is the first statement of the kind to which I have ever listened—from a man who speaking as he did at Ipswich on behalf of 17,000 labourers, at any rate is entitled, I think, to our respectful consideration ; and he said this : " Yes, if you will allow the labourers to share in your profits, they will share in your losses too." Now, I think that that was a manly and outspoken statement to make. The partners who go in are each entitled to know what the position of the others is going to be. An equal position it is and must be ; but this advantage the labourers will always get out of it : that so long as the land is cultivated at all, until we are really driven off the soil by the very extremity of the cheapness of everything we produce, so long will the labourer get some wages at any rate. Whether we get rents or you get profits, the labourer, at any rate, is certain to get such wages as will ensure the land being cultivated until the moment that we give it up.

Our Programme.

Well, gentlemen, I have been asked this : I have been asked what is the programme of this Union. Now, I myself hope that I have made it clear that this is not my Union at all ; it is yours. Therefore I do not assume the responsibility—it is no part of my duty—to hamper you beforehand with any programme upon which I do not know that all agriculturists in this country are absolutely united. I have no right to do so. If I were to put upon that programme an item which I knew divided the agricultural interest from top to bottom—and there are some which do—how could I ask those who I knew were opposed to that being carried out to join the Union at all ? And if they did not, how then would it be a National Agricultural Union in which all interests would be equally represented ?

Items of the Programme: Local Rates.

There are three items—nay, there are four, there are five—at this moment which figure in the programme of that Union. First of all there is the great question of local taxation. The incidence of local taxation upon the land is grievous, unfair, unjust, un-English, and it ought to be remedied. (Loud cheers.) I went so fully into that question at York, that, fearful as I am of taking up too much of your time, I dare not do more than indicate it now. But if those who desire to know in what way the burdens upon land could, in my humble opinion, be both easily and safely removed to the proper shoulders, will do me the honour to glance at my speech at York, they will see that the question is there treated very fully. And, audacious as the proposal that I made there was, I have been looking in vain yet for any newspaper in the country that has attempted to controvert it. Therefore, gentlemen, I say that we have a great chance, if we adopt this Union, of removing from our own shoulders to those of the community—we still bearing, of course, our fair share of the burden—those local rates which now press with such unjust weight upon agriculture. I mean such taxes as the land tax, the poor rate, the education rate, and possibly others. I have shown how they might very easily be altered without doing any injustice to anyone, and without disturbing that complicated system of assessment which, I am told, has driven one Chancellor of the Exchequer after another mad when they think of how they are going to alter it.

Disease.

There is another subject item in this programme. Your Chairman has alluded to the fact that we desire still further, if we can, to keep disease from our flocks and our herds. And that is a question which interests you here very much as a meat-producing and milk-producing country, and I trust that it is one which we shall be able to give united expression upon in a practical form as soon as ever this Agricultural Union is formed. I am quite certain that there will be no division of opinion upon it, and therefore I pass to other, not more important, but, perhaps, more controversial subjects.

Co-operation.

One of the most important things that I wish to establish in this Union is a system of co-operation between consumer and producer in order to stop, not the fair, but the unfair profits of the middleman—(cheers)—because at the present moment those profits are such that they constitute not only a fair but an excessive reward for his trouble in distributing our profits; and here I frankly say what I said at York, that you cannot get rid, advantageously to yourselves, of the middleman. He is a better distributor than you are. He knows that business, and we know ours, and if he will keep to a fair share of the profits, by all means, with my hearty goodwill, he shall have them. But I do say that, at the present moment, when we find that we are producing stock and corn absolutely at a loss, it is quite fair, and it is quite right, that we should address ourselves to the problem of whether or not those profits are fair, or whether we are not losing what ought really to belong to ourselves. I think that we are. I showed in my speech at York that in the case of one great bread company they are dividing 30 per cent. on their capital, with a bonus of 7½ per cent. added; and the chairman of that company had the frankness, I believe, to admit that the reason was that the price of wheat was very low, but that fortunately the consumer could be induced to give very nearly the same price for bread that he did when wheat was high. (Cheers.) I shall show you in two minutes how we are going to get back some part of that unfair and unequal profit. Then, gentlemen, take a thing that comes nearer home to you at the present moment; I mean the production of meat. I have been challenged in the newspapers as to a statement that I made at York, on the authority of a friend of mine who heard it from a middleman himself. I am told that it is not possible that any man should have made a profit of £200,000 by buying Canadian beef and selling it as English. Very well, Sir, then what did I do on the first public occasion on which it was brought before me? In the next speech I made, namely, at Winchester, I stated that I withdrew that statement, and that I apologised for the middleman who had made it : because it was not a statement that I made on my own responsibility, but it was one which I made on the responsibility that I quoted.

I do not believe for a moment that it was an intentionally untrue statement. I believe that, probably, he was thinking of all the profit that he had made by selling New Zealand meat as English for a long series of years, and therefore the profits got mixed up at the moment, but at present I will make the middlemen a present of that statement after withdrawing it. It will be of some advantage to them, because I find that, whenever an exaggerated statement is made, even on the responsibility of someone else, the people who gain by it are the attacked and not the attacking party. Therefore let them use that slight advantage, but let them use it with moderation, because it is not a question so much of the actual number of pounds that any particular man did or did not make. The question is—and it is one which we will probe to the core, and the more that this question is brought before me the deeper will I probe it—whether the middleman in the meat trade at the present moment is making a fair or an unfair profit upon what he sells or not. (Cheers, and a voice : "Ask your own friend, Sir, on the platform, that is with you. He is the gentleman who can supply figures and explain it to you.") Well, Sir, my own friends on the platform will have an opportunity of making any explanation they like, including the gentleman who has just addressed me.

A Farmer's Experiment.

But let me put it to you in this way. When a producer gets almost as much for the article he produces as the consumer has to pay, the only thing being deducted being a fair distributor's profit, then the middleman is making a fair profit. When the farmer is getting from 3d. to 4d., as he is doing—I do not know how it is here : I hope he is getting more, but it is so in other parts of England—(a laugh)—a gentleman laughs. He may think it a laughing matter as a farmer. I do not think it a laughing matter at all, when I have to sell my stock at less than it costs me to produce it. (Laughter and cheers.) However, I have plenty of illustrations, and every time I hear a thing of that sort I will produce one of them. What has happened on my own property, and to a man whom I do know ? He is a tenant himself, and he has attempted all through the summer to sell his sheep at a profit, and he has failed ; and at last he said, "Well, I won't be humbugged any longer. I am going to take this matter into my own hands." He sent his boy round with a cart to get orders from different villages. He got a butcher, and he paid him to kill the sheep, and from that moment he has been going on doing it week by week, and upon those very sheep which he could not sell in the market without a loss to himself as a producer, he has made a net profit of £5 a week since he began to do this himself. (Loud and continued cheers.)

Now, Sir, I do ask whether people want any more of the cards I have got up my sleeve or not; but, at any rate, this is what we shall do. We shall not do away with the middleman. (A voice : Why ?) I have already said why. I am sure that there is no cause for the susceptibility of my friend on my right. We want to leave the middleman his fair profits, and I always think that in (I am afraid) a very long speech it is necessary to say the same thing about four times before anybody will believe it. I believe that I said that four times in my speech at York. Perhaps I ought to have said it five. If so, I am sorry I did not ; but there it is, all written down, and the fair middleman is not at all attacked. We desire to leave him in possession of his fair profits. (Cheers.) Gentlemen, if anyone will get up in this room and say that he himself is an unfair middleman, then he might take a position contrary to the one I take up. (Laughter and cheers.) Otherwise he cannot do it.

Now, what we shall do is this. We propose to establish co-operative branches in the great centres of industry all over the country. Hitherto co-operative stores have meant this : they have meant the protection of the consumer. The Stores, for instance, in London, enable you and me to go and buy things more cheaply, perhaps, than we can get them elsewhere, but they are very hard on the producer. They are enormous buyers in the home market, and the policy which they pursue is this. They go into the market, and say, "It is a big order, and if you do not let us have a liberal discount we will place it elsewhere." What is that but grinding down the producer to the very lowest point which he can bear ? These great stores, then, are not in favour of the producer, but in favour of the consumer.

The Producer's Claim.

Now, what we want to do is, to produce a real system of co-operation which shall be fair to both; but if there is an advantage to be obtained, it

"The NATIONAL AGRICULTURAL UNION CABLE"

A WEEKLY NEWSPAPER.

For Landowners, Farmers, Labourers, and all interested in the Prosperity of Agriculture.

Edited by the EARL OF WINCHILSEA.

SUBSCRIPTION FORM.

Which should be filled up and returned to Lord Winchilsea at the

Offices of "The National Agricultural Union Cable,"
30, FLEET STREET,
LONDON, E.C.

I shall be glad to become a Subscriber to *"The National Agricultural Union Cable."* Annual Subscription (Post Free), **6s. 6d.**

Name_____

Address_____

Any offers of help in making the Paper known will be gladly received   The first number will be published shortly.

ought to be obtained by the producer, because I must say this —and I have said it before—that I think that we have heard a little too much of the consumer in this country. We want to hear a little more of the producer. (Cheers.) When working men talk about the interests of the consumers, do they forget that they themselves, if they are working men at all, daily produce a great deal more than they consume? Do they forget that their interests are those of producers, and not merely of consumers? Because if they do, it is just as well that that truth should be brought home to them without delay. But the men in these co-operative societies of the Union will be able to join to protect the interests of the producer, at the same time being perfectly fair to the consumer. And how can you do that and yet secure the middleman his fair profit? I will tell you.

Depots.

What we should do is to establish these depôts in different parts of the country where the producer can send his produce, and where the consumer can buy it ; and we shall publish the prices which are obtained by the producer and given by the consumer in those centres, so that they will be all over the country. Therefore, a producer, when he takes his stock to sell, will be able to say " I will not sell you for 6s. what I find I can get 7s. 6d. for at the co-operative over there." And the consumer, on the other hand, will be able to say to the middleman who supplies him, " You shall have your fair profit the same as the stores get, but I will not buy for 10s. what I can get for 9s. 6d. there." That is how we shall do it.

Lord Winchilsea as an Editor.

How shall we publish this all over the country ? Now I must assume an attitude of the deepest modesty, more especially in the presence of the gentlemen whom I see sitting below me, because I am about to unfold a secret. The way in which these anunciations will be made, or one way at any rate, will be by—let me cover my blushes, gentlemen—a weekly paper which I am going to edit myself. (Laughter and cheers.) I feel all the diffidence of a crab when it first emerges from its shell. I ask for a little kind consideration for a few weeks until my shell gets hard. I have tried two of the different estates of the realm. I have been first in the House of Commons. Now I am in the other House. Soon I am going to join the fourth estate of the realm. I shall be " our contemporary."

A Private Wire.

Well, I will promise you one thing, gentlemen, that if I can help it the paper shall not be a dull one. Perhaps it may surprise some here to know that for some years I have had my own " special wire." I can work it myself.

"Our Special Artist."

And I have also got a special artist who will weekly give you a very good cartoon. But also, perhaps, I am peculiarly fitted for this post, because I can not only write shorthand, which will not in the least surprise my friends below me, because anybody can write it, but their admiration, I am sure, will reach almost the point of incredulity, when I tell them that I can read my own notes when I have written them. (Great laughter.) Well, gentlemen, you will read that " owing to the enormous progress of this movement we have found it necessary to bring out a new organ." It is quite true. I ask in passing for your indulgence for this new organ, and I tell you that you will find it useful and not dull. (A voice : The name of it ?) The name of the paper, which my friend on my right, who is just going to subscribe to it, asks me for, will be " The National Agricultural Union Cable,"

E

and as he is so very business-like, I will tell him that he can have it for
6s. 6d. a year.

Lord Winchilsea a Universal Free Trader.

But to return to the programme. You may ask me—and if the time was
not so late I would answer it fully—why a question in which you take such
an interest, as you do perhaps in the question of Protection and Free Trade,
finds no place on this programme. I have answered that before by saying
that I dare not place there any question upon which agriculturists are
divided. It will be for the National Agricultural Union itself to take whatever line recommends itself to the majority of its members. But with regard
to 'my individual opinion, I said eleven years ago what I say now, that I
believe the true answer to this question is to be found in a universal Free
Trade, to be obtained by means of imperial federation. (Cheers.) What I mean is
this. As you know, those who were primarily responsible for recommending
Free Trade to this country thought at the time that the whole world would
adopt it. That is a matter of history. Rightly or wrongly, whether to our
interest or not, the whole world has not gone in for it. Very far from that.

Imperial Federation.

But I want to point out for one moment the imperial aspect of the question.
You have in your Empire the greatest lever in the world for opening the
ports of every country to your commodities, for doing away—and I trust that
some day it may be found quite possible—with every custom house in the
world. How can you do that? Why, by forming with your Colonies a great
federation for defence and for trade. (Cheers.) You can get from your
Colonies every single thing you want in perfect abundance, and as good and
as cheap as you can get it from anywhere else. Do not believe the contrary.
You can get it from your Colonies, and therefore you can say to other nations,
"You keep our goods out of your markets, as you are doing by the McKinley
tariff;"—and, gentlemen, I may tell you that, rightly or wrongly, 20,000 men or
more in our great manufacturing cities in England are out of work on account of
that tariff. I say that what you will be able to say to America will be this: "If
you do not admit our goods as freely as we admit yours we will put a retalia-
tory duty upon you." (Loud cheers.) Wheat would come in just the same as it
does now from India and Australia. India governs the price of wheat, because it
can be produced more cheaply there than anywhere else. It would not raise
the price of wheat, but there would be such a movement among the farmers
of the United States that no Government could stand for six weeks. They
would say, "We have grown our corn. We must send it to England. You
must take off these duties."

I saw the other day a man who had come back from Holland, and he said,
"You do not know the position of England, and how all our markets depend
upon your country; but if you were even to threaten to shut us out, you would
bring us to our knees in ten days." (Cheers.) I say that there is no country
in the world which would keep its ports closed for six months against the
United British Empire of Free Trade. Let me ask you this pertinent
question. Who would be likely to gain more, even from a selfish point of
view, than the town of Plymouth by a system of imperial trade and defence?
At the present moment it is notorious that we have not ships enough to
protect our Colonies. The moment there was a great war we should have to
leave them to protect themselves, which means that they would have no
protection at all; but if they came in on the basis of finding part of the
money for imperial defence, what does that mean but building a great many
ships? And where are they to be built if not at Plymouth? It is not in
every town in the Empire that there are docks capable of laying down a
great man-of-war. We should want a number of ships which would keep

the dockyards of Plymouth occupied during this generation at least. I do not put it to you merely, of course, from that selfish point of view, though everybody has a right to consider the interests of his own town ; but I put it to you as a great imperial answer to the question of Protection or Free Trade. I say, Yes: universal Free Trade all over the world ; and to obtain that, a federation of the British Empire. (Cheers.)

Tobacco and Free Trade.

But you may say to me, "Yes, Free Trade; but have we not got it in this country already? Well, I said at York, "Sow an acre of your own land with tobacco, and sell it, and you will very soon find out whether this is a Free Trade country or not."

Tea Duty.

There is another point. Do we impose no duty upon tea? We do, gentlemen, for the purposes of revenue ; so we are told. Well, but that wounds my conscience as a Free Trader. How can I call myself a Free Trader, and still impose a duty upon tea? But, if I do impose a duty, why in the world cannot I impose it upon something which would help the home producer? (Cheers.) What earthly benefit is it to anybody in this hall, who is producing in this country, to put a duty upon tea? And, why could not you take the duty off tea, for instance, which is as much a necessary to the working classes as bread is at this moment, and put it upon foreign fruit and vegetables, and things of that kind, which you do grow here, and therefore obtain some good by it? Perhaps it would give you the turn of the market, which at any rate is worth having. Why should the duty be imposed in a way which does you no good whatever ? It would take nothing more out of the pockets of the consumers of this country, and it would put a very great deal into yours, if the duty were so re-arranged.

Beer Duty.

One more point upon this question—the beer duty. We pay at ˙thi⁸ moment, Free Traders as we are, 6s. 3d. a barrel duty—yes, duty, upon every barrel of beer which is made, and by that 6s. 3d., though it amounts to an enormous revenue, the producers of what ought to be the ingredients of beer in this country, barley and hops, get nothing whatever. The consumer pays the whole of it, and we get no good by it.

Why in the world, if we are going to have duty for revenue purposes, can we not put it on something which would secure at any rate that beer was made of English barley and hops? (Cheers.) I know by the feeble cheers that greet that statement, that you are not a beer drinking people about here. (Laughter.) If you had heard the cheers which greeted it at Ipswich, if you had seen everybody's face expand, as if the sun had come out in his strength when I mentioned the question, then I think that you would have seen that it is not a matter which is indifferent to the working classes of this country. If that was done, the consumer would pay no more than he does now. Many an English farmer who cannot grow wheat at a profit would leave off growing it, and grow more barley, which he could grow at a profit. Many a county now, like Kent and Sussex, which used to employ thousands at the hop growing time, from London and other great towns, thus giving them a mouthful of fresh country air which did them all a world of good, besides finding them employment, would be able to do it again ; and let me tell you, gentlemen, that the beer which would be produced from those articles, would be far less likely to disagree with you or me than it does now. (Cheers.)

"Agitators."

Now, gentlemen, allow me for a moment to sum up what I have said

I think that I have pointed out to you that the crisis has not been exaggerated, and that even if you in the West of England are not feeling the full effects of it, there are reasons why you ought to join heartily with your fellow agriculturists. I have pointed out that it is a matter in which town and country are equally interested ; and I have shown you a simple, and I hope fair, method by which, without dividing any interests or attacking any fair trader—I do not use it in its technical sense, but I mean anybody who trades fairly—we can combine the great agricultural interests so as to obtain for you and for me something of that relief which we all so urgently demand. The matter now is in your hands. I have been called an agitator in this matter, but I am not careful to answer that. John Wesley was called an agitator when he preached in this country, but if his advice had been followed, the Church of England at this moment would have had many loyal sons who are now estranged from her. (Cheers.)

The Eddystone.

I saw as I came along here a very interesting monument—perhaps one of the most interesting monuments which exist—of human courage, foresight, and ingenuity. I mean that lighthouse which now is on the Hoe, but which, for one hundred and twenty years, lighted the entrance to Plymouth Sound on the Eddystone Rock. Before that building was erected 'there was another, but it failed, and why ? Because the great principles upon which alone success could have attended the endeavour were disregarded. Because if you want to place on that rock a lighthouse which will defy the elements, and last for all time, you must not only found it deep in the rock itself, but you must also take care that the building itself is composed of the same durable material.

In my humble way I have attempted here to follow the example rather of that lighthouse which is now erected as a trophy on the Hoe, than of that one in which the gallant inventor so unfortunately himself perished, by a disregard of the principles by which alone he could have commanded success. I have taken advantage of a spring tide—and our affairs are at a very low ebb at this moment—to examine the bed rock, and I have found a solid foundation in the fact that our interests are the same. I have taken care in building upon this rock to place on it, in every tier, as it were, of the building, three great stones, dovetailed together, one representing the interests of each of the classes engaged in agriculture.

I have not cared whether or not I had to abandon that work for a time, while the tide of criticism rose and surged around it, directed perhaps in some cases by those who, with a true wrecker's instinct, aimed at spoiling the project. I have gone back when it has subsided, and found that the building has only been cleaned and beautified by the waves which have gone over it, because it was not only founded upon a rock, but built on principles which cannot be assailed. I will carry that building on, if you will allow me, to the point at which it will be safe from the waves around it. It will be for you, then, to take up the work, and on the same principle to add tier after tier to the building, until, at length, it sheds forth from its summit a light which shall shine far and wide over the waters of human life, and shall, if Heaven so wills, guide into harbour many a poor agricultural bark which, but for its saving beams, would have gone down and perished in the waters. (Loud cheers.)

SPEECH

Rt. Hon. the EARL of WINCHILSEA & NOTTINGHAM,

Delivered in the Corn Exchange, Bedford, on Saturday,
January 28th, 1893.

THE MAYOR OF BEDFORD IN THE CHAIR.

THE EARL OF WINCHILSEA AND NOTTINGHAM said: Mr. Mayor, you, Sir have infused into this meeting something of a difference between it and other meetings which I have been privileged to address. You are the Mayor of a large and important town, and in your position you have seen that the interests committed to your charge, the interests of this town, are absolutely identical with those of the great industry to which many of us here belong—agriculture, and therefore you have taken the very wise step of calling us here together, partly to show how much you sympathise yourself with the condition agriculture is in, and partly to teach us this lesson—and it will be well if our audience will take it to heart—that the interests of town and country are one and the same wherever the great national industry, agriculture, is attacked. (Cheers.) There is another point which I notice with great interest. When the Mayor first called this meeting together he called it in a general way, I believe, to discuss the crisis in agriculture, but when it came to the practical point of what should be discussed it was seen and recognised that it was not of so much use to demonstrate the conditions under which we are suffering as it was to discuss what is, so far as I know, the only practical remedy which has been proposed, and upon which we are all agreed, and therefore it was that this meeting was turned from one for a general discussion upon the crisis to one to discuss the practical scheme which I have laid before the country for bringing about a better state of things in that great industry, and I rejoice, gentlemen, to find as I go about the country and attempt to explain this scheme, that every meeting at which I am privileged to explain it contains more and more people who understand the position before I begin.

The Scheme Making its Way.

That shows me that the scheme is making its way among thoughtful people in the country. The remarks which the Mayor addressed to you show that he, at any rate, has seized completely the principles which I wish to bring before you. Gentlemen, what is the condition of things to which the Mayor has alluded? Is it true that we want a remedy and an instant one? I am asked why I am in such a hurry in this matter. Why do I go all over the country from one meeting to another instead of waiting until the ordinarily constituted associations can hold a meeting, first, at the end of January, and then another at the end of February, and another in March, and so on. I say I do it because the thing admits of no delay. (Cheers.) I say I do it because there are thousands of poor fellows whose heads will go under water if we do not bring them some remedy, and very soon. (Cheers.) If that is true, gentlemen, of the exertions I have been attempting to make in their behalf, it is true also that it is your duty to help me and see whether there is not something in this scheme which will be of practical value, and if there is leave it no longer in my hands, but when you leave this room, leave it with the intention to do all you can to impress upon the people of this country the absolute need of some such organisation as that which I wish to bring before you. Before we can discuss the remedy, we must have one word as to the cause.

Foreign Competition.

No doubt the Conference in London was right when it attributed the cause of our depression in a very great measure to foreign competition. (Cheers.) There is no doubt that the very low prices which we get for everything that we produce prevents the farmer from making the profit from the sale of his produce which he can do when prices are good. That runs through the whole of the agricultural industry at the present moment —so much so that prices have touched a level in many cases which do not come up to the cost of production. That is perfectly true, but that is the natural cause. You can never do away with foreign competition. I am not disposed—taking a wider outlook, perhaps, than the farmer—entirely to quarrel with it, because what it has done is this, at any rate it has provided the people of this country with plenty of good cheap food, and that is a thing which no one who loves his country can look upon with indifference, but when we come to consider the particular effect it has had upon the agricultural industry, it is perfectly true that the depression under which we are labouring must—it is a matter of accounts—be due very much to the fact that we are getting very low prices for what we sell, and that these prices are very much due to the foreign stuff coming in at a price at which we here can hardly produce the articles we have to sell. (Cheers.) That is a cause which we can never hope entirely to do away with, nor can we wish entirely to do away with it.

Party Politics.

Let me say, as your Chairman has told you, that this is a question which has nothing whatever to do with party politics. I am pleased to see gentlemen on the platform of all shades of political opinions. When we say that this is not a party question, of course we do not mean that no party person is to engage in it; otherwise our platform would be perfectly empty. What we mean is that persons of all parties are to come into it and give us their advice and assistance—so that when at Ipswich we had a Conservative candidate in the chair and the Radical member moving the resolution, it was pleasing to me because I could say, " Whichever of you gets in, the interests of the Union are safe." (Laughter.) From that point of view I should desire particularly the presence here of the member who has the honour of representing this constituency. I should like to have heard, and should respectfully have listened to, any suggestions that he might have made. He was unable to come, but he has sent you a letter, which has been read from the chair, and so far as his suggestions are concerned, namely, making the transfer of land cheaper, securing to the tenant his reasonable rights, and giving the labourer more direct interest in the soil he cultivates, I am perfectly with him. I have said so before, and I should have convinced him if he had been here, that it is by joining this Agricultural Union that precisely these objects can be obtained ; but when the hon. member goes on to say that agricultural distress has its origin in natural causes and cannot be wholly cured by human law, I say, gentlemen, that that is a counsel which I am not willing to receive. (Cheers.) There may be natural causes, but we as Englishmen are accustomed in all parts of the world to combat natural causes and to overcome them. However natural may be the causes which at present afflict our industries, it is still more natural to us as Englishmen to strive against them —yes, and overcome them. (Cheers.) What should we think of a doctor who went to the bedside of a patient and said, "You are suffering from natural causes, and there is nothing that I can do?" (Laughter.)

Natural Causes and Artificial Remedies.

Gentlemen, we are suffering from natural causes, but natural causes have also artificial remedies, and some of these remedies we wish to apply. But I must say when the hon. member goes on to say that he cannot be a party to any legislation which, however remotely, would increase the price of bread, I think he is hardly, if I may venture to say so, dealing fairly with my scheme. (Cheers.) There is not a single word in any speech which I have delivered in which there is any such policy indicated. I have stated that Protection is not upon the programme of the Union, that so far as my individual opinions are concerned I stand exactly where I did thirteen years ago, that I am a universal free trader, and believe in imperial federation as the lever by which it is to be furthered. And inasmuch as I have sent a copy of my speech at York, containing all this, to every member of the House of Commons, I can only regret that those numerous engagements of which your member speaks, and which have prevented him being present, have also prevented him apparently having had time to read that speech. (Laughter.) But the matter does not stop there as far as agriculture is concerned. Natural causes there are, and I have alluded to them.

Artificial Causes.

But there are also artificial causes, and these we shall first and most successfully attack. One of those causes is to be found in the fact that other great interests in this country are organised and that we are not. Therefore competition, coming as it does upon a disorganised interest, has enabled everybody to take an advantage of us, which they would not have done if you and I were organised to resist them. Will anyone tell me that the increased railway rates are natural causes? (Laughter.) Will anybody tell me that the fact that while land and houses only come in for one-sixth of the whole income of the country, yet they are charged almost the whole of the local taxation; is that a natural cause? (Cheers.) Will anyone tell me that when I go into the market and get 3d. or 4d. a pound for meat, and when I come back shortly afterwards as a consumer and have to pay for the same meat 9d. or 10d. a pound, that that is a natural cause? (Laughter.) No, gentlemen, these are artificial causes, and they are the very causes that are making the difference between profit and loss in the business in which we are engaged, and I would suggest that, however interesting natural causes may be that cannot be removed, more interest still attaches—and especially to the member representing a division like this—to artificial causes which can and ought to be removed. (Cheers.) Well, now, on that ground I shall hope, particularly after what I have said of those three remedies he proposes, to find in your member a staunch adherent of the National Agricultural Union. (A voice: What about Lord Carrington's system?) I know something about that, for it is not very different to the one I have pursued for many years on my own estate.

Causes of the Depression.

I will come to that if you like, but what we are dealing with now is the great question of what are the causes which have led to the present position, and I am pointing out first of all competition, and secondly disorganisation, which has led to the railways increasing their rates, to the local taxation of the country being placed almost entirely on our shoulders, and to the middle-man taking not the fair profit which we all desire to leave in his hands, but a share of the profit which is now so large as to turn into a loss the business of producing meat and corn in this country. (Cheers.) What is the remedy that I propose for this state of things? Simply to organise ourselves into a great National Agricultural Union.

Principles of the Union.

And let me tell you first the principles on which we are going to do it. If it were not the case that the interests of the three classes were the same in this matter, then I think we should find it impossible to get them to unite in one and the same Union. Therefore it is very important that we should make up our minds first of all what those interests are, and whether they are identically the same. Is our depression due to the fact that profits have vanished from the land altogether; that in many cases land is going out of cultivation, rents have ceased to be paid, profits have ceased to be made, and we are even coming to a point when there is no money left to pay the wages of the labourers?

Organisation.

I say when we get to that point we want organisation in which we can all join. Our interests are exactly the same; for what is the interest of every class connected with the land? Why, to restore to it the gains it has lost, out of which alone either of the three classes obtain rent, profit, or wages. As I said, when agriculture is prosperous, you may possibly disagree as to the division of profits; but now, when profits have ceased to trouble us by disappearing altogether, our first duty as men of business and sense is to join together to restore those profits to the land, without which we cannot live. (Cheers.) But we must make sure that each class who joins the Union will find its interests taken care of in the Union we propose to establish.

Landlords' Interests.

Take first of all my own class. What are our interests? The interest of the landlord, I suppose, is to have good tenants upon his estate, good comfortable cottages for his labourers, and contented occupants in them. I don't think I can put it more plainly than that. It is certainly not the interest of the landlord to farm his own land. (Laughter.) That I know from experience. It must be his interest to have it farmed by somebody else. I am certain every landlord here will bear me out when I say that his interest lies in the direction of having a tenantry, free as air if you will, to carry out, according to their own brains and intellect, improvements in the soil in which their capital is invested. I am perfectly certain that if there is any modification of the Agricultural Holdings Act that can be suggested which would make the tenant more secure, which would make it more certain that he would get back that which he had put into the soil, it is as much the interest of the landlord as of the tenant that such a provision should be put into the Act.

Tenant Farmers' Interests.

I hope one of the first things the National Agricultural Union does will be to take up this question from the point of view of the tenant farmer. (Cheers.) I have put that in the forefront, but since the meeting at Ipswich I have been told by one or two tenant armers that I gave more prominence to the views of the labourers than to theirs. That is not so. You will remember that I was announced to speak at Ipswich specially to the labourers, and it was my duty to address the greater part of my remarks to those who had done me the honour of coming to hear what I had to say. It does not follow that I think less of the interests of the tenants or land-lords. On the contrary, I have always before me the interest of the three classes, and my wish is that on every council and committee of the National Agricultural Union each of the three classes shall find itself fairly and equally represented. (Cheers.)

Labourers' Interests.

What is the interest of the labourer? That is an extremely important point, because I may remind you that unless you get the labourer to act with you in this matter you cannot carry any useful point. The interests of the labourer are, I think, first of all to get good permanent work, and good fair wages. That is the great mainstay to which he ought to look. There are other things which can be brought about for his benefit, and which the National Agricultural Union will be a great instrument in effecting. As I see many labourers present, I will give a short sketch of what I mean when I say that while good wages and permanent employment are the labourers' mainstay, there are other things which can be got for him, and which will increase the happiness of his life.

First, there is the question of allotments. Many years before the labourers had votes at all, they had allotments at fair rents on my own property. (Cheers.) I think it is manifest to every person of common sense that the only spare capital of the labourer is his spare time. Very well. If he has a broken day, it is to everybody's advantage, and especially to the advantage of the labourer himself, that he should have an allotment on which he can work as near to his own cottage as it can conveniently be. (Cheers.) And, gentlemen, I do think that some landlords—I do not say all —make a mistake when they charge a higher price for allotments than they charge for farm land. (Hear, hear, and cheers.) Of course, it is a little more trouble to collect the rents; and of course you have to pay rates and taxes upon them, and it is fair to add that. Nobody would suggest that this is not fair, but I do think that the little cost of collection ought not to be taken into account when weighed against the great a vantage you give to the working classes by giving these allotments. (Cheers.) One hundred years ago my ancestor of the same name gave this evidence before a Royal Commission. He said, "On my estate in Rutland I have ninety of these small holders, and they are the best tenants I have got. They pay the rents, and do themselves more good than any others." (Cheers.)

There is a further point, one more step upon the ladder, in which we take the greatest interest, and in which I think you will bear me out when I say, that if the landlords and tenants of England will really make up their minds to do so, they can do more for you in six months than you can get in ten years by any amount of legislation. (Cheers.) What I want to see is not that they should turn their backs one on the other. I want them to turn round and look one another in the face. I want to see these two classes, who have the power, set themselves to do what many of the tenants have done. and take the labourer by the hand, and see if they cannot give him something which, if he is an enterprising and honest fellow who wants to make his way, will lift him gradually up by his own exertions.

Labourers Rise by their Own Exertions.

I believe the labourers would rather rise by their own exertions than by anything in the way of charity, whether public or private. They know that every step so gained is solid ground. And if he is not prevented, by those who have the power, from doing it, and has a free hand, there are many means by which the labourer can do so. I can only indicate one more to you before I leave this part of the subject. On my estate what we have done is this : We have many cottages in one village with five acres of grass land attached to them. The labourers work for wages themselves, and their wives and families look after the stock, so that they have two strings to their bow. Then they go on from five acres to ten, and so on. Now, I say that a system of that kind, carefully thought out, is far better than any legislation by which you are to have land and rent it from the State—one of the very worst landlords, I believe, you could possibly have—(cheers)— because it would not be able, it would be contrary to its public duty, to give you any reduction of rent in a bad time. If you can get land on these conditions, I honestly believe it is far better than following the will-o'-the-wisps which are dangled before us at certain times of political excitement. But the labourers will say, and they are perfectly entitled to say, " The last time prices were really high we did not get the share we ought to have had. Our wages were low when prices were high, and what guarantee do you offer—how can you make me certain—that if I join you and help to get these taxes off the land, and help to bring back prosperity, that that may not mean prosperity for you, and not for me ? " (Cheers.) That is what they ask, and they say, " What is the guarantee we have that if we go into this thing with you we shall each have a fair share of what is gained ? " We do it in this way. We go back to the great principle which I first of all laid down—that all our interests are the same, and that we are three people engaged in the same business—the labourer, the farmer, and the landlord.

Division of Profits.

I say in principle you are entitled to divide the fair profits of that industry among yourselves equally. (Cheers.) And when I say that, I do not mean what is known as profit sharing—that is to say, that your books are to be open to be looked at every Saturday night. What I mean is, that we are to adopt that great principle in going into the Union. We do not interfere with individual bargains between man and man, but we appeal to that principle as the right one in dividing the profits, and I suggested at Ipswich that a sliding scale of wages should be adopted according to the price of agricultural produce. That is not a new idea, nor really different to what prevails at present. What happened last year when corn went up to 40s. a quarter ? Immediately my labourers came to me and said they must have more wages, which I gave them. That was nature calling for a sliding scale. Corn went up in value, and everybody saw wages ought to rise. A sliding scale of rent would be much more difficult ; we must leave that between man and man. What do you think will happen supposing the price of everything goes down ? The tenant will go to his landlord and say that as prices have gone down he wants something taken off his rent. If the landlord is a fair dealing man, he will take a proper percentage off the rent; and if he does not, he ought to. (Cheers, and a voice, " They are very few.") By this National Agricultural Union, if they be few, we will convert them into many. And if the landlord does not do that, he would not be treating the other two partners fairly in the matter if, when the price of things goes down, he does not reduce rent in proportion. [A Voice : " The landlords have the cream, and always will."] (Laughter.) That is not proper, and I would divide the cream equally between the three classes. (Cheers.) And they could share the skim milk too if they liked. (Laughter.) The more you tell me that landlords take the cream, the more ought you to come into the National Agricultural Union, and then you would render it difficult for them, if not impossible.

Separate Organisations Useless.

Now I should like to point this out, because perhaps my friend might think that a remedy is to be found in a different direction. You may say, " We will organise for our own class. We will have a labourers' organisation. We will have a tenant farmers' organisation, and you can have a landlords' organisation or not," I suppose you would say, "as you like." There is no idea of a landlords' organisation, and therefore I will take the other two as separate organisations. Well, now, I have stated already that in the National Agricultural Union we propose to do justice between man and man, that the tenant should have a fair security for his investments, and that all the three partners, as it were, should be treated equally. But now supposing that we are going to ask for what is fair and right, and you propose to attain it by a separate organisation. What would be your means of getting what you wanted ? I am told that, like every great organisation, you would be represented in the House of Commons, and have tenant farmer representatives ready to carry out your commands. Gentlemen, when you talk of tenant farmers in the House of Commons, remember this : that under present political conditions there is not a single constituency in England where, if the tenant farmers separate themselves from the labourers, they could return a member to the House of Commons. (Hear, hear.) This is not pleasant hearing for a great many people, but I stand here to tell you the truth whether it is pleasant or not.

Representation of the Three Classes.

But I do say this, that if you go into this organisation with the other two classes, we can return some tenant farmer members to the House of Commons, and then one could be exceedingly glad to see them there, because they would not be representing the narrow interests of one class, but they would be part of the great representation of all the three classes engaged in agriculture. It would be fair then that the labourers should join you in electing some tenant farmer members, because you prove by going into the National Agricultural Union that your interests are the same as theirs, and if you do I believe they will prove that they think their interests are the same as yours by voting every now and then for a representative who is a tenant farmer. If that is the case, gentlemen, let me ask you whether it is not better even from a selfish point of view to join an organisation of the three classes, which can effect this, sooner than to confine yourself to an organisation of one class which really without the other two can effect nothing ? Let me take this other point, and let me impress this upon the labourers who are present here. We have had before separate labour organisations. We had some years ago—I don't know if it came to this county, but it came to Lincolnshire—a Union which had a very right object. The object was to endeavour to get a sliding scale of wages. At that time wheat was about 60s. a quarter, and the labourers thought they ought to have 3s. a day. They made their organisation, not in concert with the other two classes, but in such a way that it was really a trial of strength between themselves and their employers. Well, they put in 2d. a week, I think, to this Union, which was to give them sick pay besides strike pay. The result of it was this: for a few weeks the wages were raised ; afterwards they fell again lower than they were before, and a great many poor fellows who had put their 2d. a week in, thinking that they would get sick pay out, lost everything that they had put into that Union—I will not say because the Union was dishonestly managed, but because the people who founded it did not know what any banker could have told them : that it was impossible on 2d. a week to obtain benefits which they proposed to give. That was the fate of the Labour Union, which was a Union of one class only against the other classes. If you will carry your minds back for a minute to those benefits which I have told you will accrue by joining the great Union which will combine the three classes, you will see what you get by your separate Labour Unions, and what you will get by this Union I propose. What is the constitution of the Union which is now proposed ? I have brought it before seven, and I think this is the eighth great public meeting in the country ; every single one of these meetings has been representative of more than one county, and yet at 'every one I have had a unanimous resolution in favour of the scheme. (Cheers.) Therefore it is making its way steadily in the public favour, and I ask you for your attention while I place it as a matter of business precisely before you. Membership of the Union 'is to be open to al¹ classes and persons interested in agriculture.

Scale of Subscriptions.

The scale of subscriptions will be different. Landlords will pay according to their acreage, and labourers will only be asked to pay one penny per month. In return for that they will be given something which I think they will like, and which will also be a very powerful weapon in the future in the hands of the Union. We propose to give them a monthly paper with good illustrations in return for their penny. So when they have got their monthly paper, if we do them no good, at any rate we shall have done them no harm. They will be quits with us, and they can watch and see what other benefits we are able to bring them.

Management of the Union.

I propose also that all the classes interested should have equal control in the management of the Union. We should have first of all a branch in every parish or group of parishes, for this reason : that the labouring man cannot be expected to go beyond the limits of his own parish in order to attend meetings. Then there will be as the next step higher the market town. The parishes will elect their delegates to the market towns, and we take the towns because they are places of business to which everybody in the neighbourhood resorts. The next unit above that is the county. The market towns will elect their delegates to the counties, and the counties will in turn elect their delegates to the central council in London. By this means there will be elected one delegate from each class, so that when you come to London you will find the Council equally divided between the classes interested in the land. How should we, then, be able to work this great Union when we have it? What we should do is this. We should send down by means of the paper of which I have told you subjects for discussion by those different branches. They would pass resolutions upon them, and they would send them up to London by their delegates, so that when the Central Council met we should be in possession of the opinion of all the members of the Union all over the country. The Council would be

The NATIONAL AGRICULTURAL UNION CABLE"

A WEEKLY NEWSPAPER,

For Landowners, Farmers, Labourers, and all interested in the Prosperity of Agriculture.

Edited by the EARL OF WINCHILSEA.

SUBSCRIPTION FORM

Which should be filled up and returned to Lord Winchilsea at the

Offices of "The National Agricultural Union Cable,"

30, FLEET STREET,
LONDON, E.C.

I shall be glad to become a Subscriber to "**The National Agricultural Union Cable.**" Annual Subscription (Post Free), **6s. 6d.**

Name

Address

Any offers of help in making the Paper known will be gladly received. The first number will be published shortly.

able to speak with the united voice of agriculture, and believe me, gentlemen, when it does so speak, there is no Government that ever will or ever has existed in this country, that could afford to neglect its voice. (Cheers.) I have been asked what the Union is to do as soon as it is formed. We must put upon our programme those things we are all agreed upon.

Local Taxation.

There is that question of local taxation, upon which I spoke before. We ought to insist upon the justice of our cause. We do not ask for any favour at the hands of the country. But what we do ask is, that burdens like the poor rate, the land tax, the education rate, and so forth, should return to be what they were at first—national burdens, to be placed upon the country at large. (Cheers.) We would contribute our fair share to them, but not the unfair share which is now crushing us so that we can hardly bear it. (Cheers.)

Increased Railway Rates.

The second thing we should do would be to protest effectively against the increased railway rates which the companies appear likely to charge for home produce. (Cheers.) I have attacked these rates before, and I am quite ready to attack them again, for they constitute, if they are not removed, in some cases an absolute barrier, as great as if you were to close the gate of a field and lock it against the exit of the produce grown there. We cannot produce against such rates, and there will be thousands of tons of excellent food all rotting in the ground because it does not pay to move it unless those rates are quickly and greatly reduced.

We talk of taxes on the food of the country, but what is that but a most unjust and iniquitous tax placed upon it by the companies, which they would not have so placed if they had known their own interests, for their interests are the same as ours. Why are they the same? Simply because we, and not the foreign producers, are always certain to use the railway, whereas the foreigner can enter one port or another. The railway cannot keep him out if he desires to go to another part of the country, but we inland are the best and most permanent customers the railways have. Therefore I rejoice very much that there are signs of the companies coming to reason. They are about to hold a meeting, at which I trust those rates will be given up; and it would not become me now to say one word of irritation, but if the companies have any difficulty when they meet, I will give them one simple and sound rule which will shorten their proceedings and please us at the same time—when they have an old and new rate, let them take whichever is the lowest, and we shall be perfectly satisfied. (Cheers.)

Producer and Consumer Together.

Next, we want in some practical way to try to bring producer and consumer together, and save some part of those unfair profits the Mayor has alluded to; but as time is flying, and I ought not much longer to occupy your attention, I will only say I believe it can be done. Figures show it can be, and if so, we may again grow at a profit if we can save the difference on what we now only grow at a loss.

Now, one word upon a question which I indicated just now as in my opinion an important and integral part of the Union. It is impossible for me or others to continue to go all over England, making speeches from time to time, and explaining the progress of the Union ; but we shall avail our-selves of the greatest engine known to modern science for doing it—I mean the Press. If you want to make this Union a great and powerful weapon in the hands of the agricultural interest, you must have a paper of your own which will tell you what is going on in the different counties, towns, and parishes, bring you into communication one with the other, and weld you all together into one whole. There is more in this proposal than in any other for welding together a great interest like the agricultural interest, scattered as it is over different parts of the country, and difficult, as we have often found it, to keep it together for one common purpose. There are many other things which I hope for from this Union, to one or two of which I will allude. There will be, of course, a good number of persons, wealthy persons, who get their wealth, not from the land, as that would not make them very wealthy at the present time, but from other things. It is to them we shall look for the subscriptions, without which the work cannot be carried on.

A Really Good Benevolent Fund.

In this Union which we propose to form there should be something which has always been wanting in every union—I mean a really good benevolent fund for the benefit of the poorer members. We should not seek to interfere with the existing friendly societies, for they do their work very well, better than we could do it for them. I well take a case of this kind. A man from illness is unable to keep up his payments to his club ; and we might keep them up for him. (Cheers.) Many instances will occur to you when you wished you had half a sovereign to give to a poor fellow who really was doing his best to keep his head above water, but failed for a time. If we could do something of that kind we should do a noble act to bind us together in the great bonds of charity—using the word charity in its highest sense. There are some other things I should like to bring before you, but I pass them over because of the time. There are, however, two things, and very important ones, which I should like to indicate.

Import Duties.

At the present moment I do not think our import duties are so imposed as to do the greatest amount of good. We impose a duty on tea, and it wounds my conscience as a free trader that we should have one. That duty does not do good to any producer, because we cannot produce tea in this country. Suppose you take the duty off tea—this duty pressing on the poorer classes—and put it on foreign fruit and vegetables; it would then be paid by the wealthier class of consumers. That would take nothing out of anybody's pocket, and it would perhaps give the home producer the turn of the market.

Beer Duty.

There is another question. At the present moment you and I are paying 6s. 3d. a barrel duty upon beer, and yet we drink stuff which really is very often not at all what it ought to be. (Cheers.) Now I wish, gentlemen, to put beer upon our programme in this sense, that we may try and get that duty altered in such a way as to secure that beer shall be made of English barley and English hops. (Cheers.) If you do that you will not be taking another farthing out of the pockets of the consumer, because he pays 6s. 3d. now. You would probably be adding something like ten shillings a quarter to the price of English barley, that would do the farmer a great deal of good, and you would get increased wages without at the same time taking a shilling out of the pockets of the consumers of the country. (Cheers.)

One of the Greatest Popular Movements.

Well, gentlemen, this is the project which I have placed before you to-night. By many who have considered it, it has been thought one of the greatest popular movements of the present day. I believe if you cordially join in carrying it out you will do much to restore the prosperity of the great industry by which you live, you will do much also to benefit the towns, which cannot thrive except by your prosperity. Take, for instance, those who are engaged in the manufacture of agricultural implements. If the soil does not pay to till, one of the greatest industries of Bedford must fall, and with it one of the most genial-hearted of your fellow citizens, because if tillage does not pay, agricultural implements will be useful for nothing that I know of except to put into a museum of antiquities. But we want to keep all these industries going. Sooner than that the plough shall be taken out of one acre now cultivated, I should like to see it going over thousands of acres now lying fallow. (Hear, hear.) I know this, that for every hundred acres which you cultivate with the plough you find employment for four labourers, whereas for every hundred acres you are obliged to let go for grass those four poor fellows go to swell the ranks of the unemployed. If, therefore, we can arouse increased interest in these matters, we shall do the nation good service, for it is high time that England should heal up her class divisions if she is to maintain the proud position she has hitherto occupied among the nations of the world.

A SPEECH

Rt. Hon. the EARL of WINCHILSEA & NOTTINGHAM,

*Delivered in the Assembly Room of the Grand Hotel, Bristol, on
Thursday, February 9th, 1893.*

THE LORD FITZHARDINGE IN THE CHAIR.

THE EARL OF WINCHILSEA AND NOTTINGHAM: Lord Fitzhardinge, Ladies, and Gentlemen, I rejoice very much to meet a great agricultural gathering like this, representative, I believe, of four counties, in an important trade centre like the city of Bristol; because I desire to impress upon the country at the very outset that in defending the cause of agriculture we are defending no selfish interest, but a national one, and that our great cites will eventually suffer equally with ourselves if agriculture, the greatest trade in the country, is suffered to be longer depressed. (Cheers.) Bristol is dependent for its prosperity, first of all, upon the imports and exports which its shipping conveys, and as the 8,000,000 people who are dependent, more or less, upon agriculture are by far the largest consumers, and the best customers that the trade of England possesses, every city like Bristol which has a great port is more, perhaps, dependent on agriculture than it is at first sight aware of; and, secondly, every great city must view with alarm the state of things which makes it more and more necessary, unfortunately, for our agricultural labourers to leave the villages in which they were born, and to crowd into large towns, seeking employment there, often finding none, and either adding to the burden of the rates, or making it more difficult than it was before for artisans to obtain remunerative employment.

Severity of the Crisis.

Your Chairman has told you much that is extremely interesting, and everything that he has said with regard to agriculture I cordially endorse. With regard to the present crisis, has it or has it not been exaggerated ? I am told that in some parts of the country agriculturists are not so much depressed as they are in others ; but none of those who attended the great conference in London, who read the papers, or are in communication with different parts of the kingdom, can fail to know and perceive that a crisis of unexampled severity is passing at this present moment over the whole industry to which we belong. (Cheers.) And if you or I have our habitation cast in favoured places, if we happen to live in some happy valley which agricultural depression has not yet touched, are we on that account to sever ourselves from the great body of our fellow agriculturists ? (A voice, "No.") "No," says a gentleman on my right, and it is the echo of the common sense of this meeting ; because I may stand on a pinnacle at this moment, but how do I know how high this tide is going to rise, and whether it may not sweep me away next ? Our only safeguard lies in common and united efforts, in order that we may rescue the whole industry by which we live from the state in which it now lies. (Cheers.)

Fair and Unfair Competition.

With one thing which was decided at the Conference I am entirely in accord, namely, that one cause of the depression under which we suffer—perhaps the greatest cause—is the general fall in prices due to foreign competition. (Loud cheers.) That cannot be denied. Whatever view we may take of foreign competition, it is unfortunately true that, whatever blessings it brings in its train, it does drive the producer of this country into a corner, for it does force him to produce, no longer at a profit, but at a loss to himself, many of those articles which he grows. (Cheers.) But there is such a thing as fair competition, and there is such a thing as unfair and fraudulent competition. Now the form of competition to which your Chairman has alluded, namely, the selling of one article under a false pretence that it is another, I distinctly brand as fraudulent. (Cheers.) I am told that in a city not a hundred miles from where we are assembled there are people who make something like £100 a week by the sale of margarine, pretending that it is butter. Every now and then they are brought before a bench of magistrates and fined £15. But you may do a very simple sum. Take an occasional £15 from £100 weekly profit, and you will find that it pays very well to go on at that game ; so that the restrictions at present imposed are utterly inadequate to put a stop to what is not fair competition at all, but a colourable pretence—selling one thing as if it was, in fact, another.

Licences to Sell Foreign Substances.

I think, as your Chairman has said, that if the Minister of ʻAgriculture wants to know what he is to do for our relief, we may call upon him first of all to enforce existing Acts more strictly. But we must also ask Parliament for a more stringent remedy. We must ask that all who sell foreign substances should be obliged to take out a licence to sell them, and that on a conviction of a fradulent transaction, such as that which I have described, whatever court had power over this matter, should be able in the first place to endorse the licence, and if the offence were repeated, to cancel and to forfeit it. (Loud cheers.) In this connection, gentlemen, we propose, and one of the first things that we desire to do is, to bring in a Bill to label foreign and colonial meat. (Cheers.) That is a proposal which I am glad to think has received the assent of numerous and important classes in this country, besides the agricultural interest. In the first place, it will benefit the producer of this country, because it will enable him then to obtain a proper price for his English product. In the next place, it will benefit the consumer who desires to purchase English meat, because he will no longer have foreign meat palmed off upon him, and be obliged to pay for it the price of English. (Cheers.) But, in the next place, it will benefit all fair middlemen in this trade, because I am told that, when they sell under its proper name, English beef or mutton, they are undersold in their own markets by persons who come and sell foreign mutton pretending that it is English, and therefore that their custtomers come to them and say, "Why cannot you sell us English beef and mutton at the same price as we can buy it in the market?" Therefore I say that such a Bill would be a protection to the middleman who desires nothing but his fair profits. Those profits nobody is more anxious that he should secure and retain than I am, because I am certain that if a middleman will keep to the fair profits of his business, though you and I are excellent producers, he is the best distributor of our produce.

Well, I have spoken of competition in its fair and its unfair form. The one we must probably make up our minds to. The other, I think, is placing a burden upon our industry which we are well entitled to ask Parliament to remove.

Disorganisation—Railway Rate

But I contend that there is a further cause for this agricultural depression beyond competition altogether, and that is the fact that you alone of all the great industries of the country are totally and absolutely disorganised. (Cheers.) What is it but this that makes you, as it were, the beast of burden for everybody who will not bear his own share of the national obligations? (Loud cheers.) Again, is it possible that the railway companies of this country would have dared to treat a great organised interest as they have just treated you and me, that they would have raised their rates in some cases by two, three, or four hundred per cent., so as to place a barrier against the transport of our produce to market as real as if they had absolutely locked it into our fields. I go further, and I say that I, being nothing at all, and you being everything, the moment that I raised my voice and ventured to speak on your behalf, on behalf of the great agricultural interest throughout this country, the railways—whether it was a coincidence or not I do not know—but they did begin to alter those rates and to say that they were not to be enforced. (Loud cheers.) That is no bad object lesson for you, for it teaches you what you can do the very minute that you threaten to organise. You are not organised yet, but the moment you say that you will, then and there other great industries of the country who have gone beyond their fair limits begin to retreat within those limits again ; and there we hope to confine them.

There is another point which shows our disorganisation, and that is the share which you and I bear of the local burdens of the country. (Loud cheers.) It would be incredible if it were not absolutely true that upon one-sixth of the income of the country, which is all that you and I nominally possess, is placed almost the whole of the local burdens of this country. It is the more incredible because it was not always so, for this nation saw, when these burdens were first imposed, that they were national burdens, and ought to be borne by the whole property of the nation at large. The poor rate and the land tax, when they were first imposed, were imposed upon all kinds of property alike; and it was only because we have been too disorganised to resist it, that other industries have shuffled out of their own share of these burdens, and have placed them entirely upon our shoulders. (Cheers.)

The Queen's Speech.

But we may come nearer home and see how the events of the last few days point the moral, and show the necessity for organising the agricultural interest. I too, like yourselves, conceived from the Queen's Speech some hopes at least, and those hopes I must say were strengthened when I heard Lord Brassey in the House of Lords, in moving the Address in reply to Her Majesty's gracious Speech, say that we might hope for some alleviation of our distress in the direction of lightening taxation.

Now, as I know that it is a very few months since, on Mr. Provand's motion, a hundred followers of the Prime Minister in the House of Commons voted for increasing the burdens on land, I must say that I regarded that as a new departure of considerable interest and some promise, and I got up immediately in my place in the House of Lords, and I pinned the noble lord to that statement.

Debate on the Address.

But what has happened since in the House of Commons ? Various amendments to the Address have been proposed. Each proposer of each amendment has taken his own line and urged his own pet remedy. We are exactly where we were before. All we have done is to enable the Minister of Agriculture to say, "You do not know what you want yourselves, and therefore I do not know what to give you" (laughter) ; and that is one result of our disorganisation.

Another result is that it enables politicians to seek these divisions and take them on purely party lines. Now, that I consider is a most pestilent state of things, because, if agriculture is to have its interests properly represented, we must have no divisions on party lines on agricultural questions. (Loud cheers.) We ought to have a consensus of opinion such as the National Agricultural Union, when you have made it what it ought to be, will be able to give expression to. We ought then to have recognised persons in charge of the sentiments of the Union, and able to express them in the House of Commons ; and we ought to have it well understood that if the Government of the day, whether it be Liberal or Conservative, will shut its eyes to our just claims, then that members from both sides of the House will join us in the division that we shall insist on taking, and will impress on the Government of the day, whoever may be in office, that agriculture is not an interest which they can safely afford to neglect.

No Party Movement.

I have said, and I repeat it, that this is no party movement. Party tactics in Parliament may be necessary for other objects, but there are great occasions on which they ought to be swept on one side ; and when the interests of a great industry like our own come into conflict with them, then I do say that those who, as your Chairman says, having been returned to Parliament by agricultural votes, assume to help agriculture in Parliament, ought to say to the Government of the day, even if they be followers of that Government, " On this matter we really must bring a little pressure to bear upon you, and we must ask you to attend to us and to give us what we want." In that policy we shall find a solution of the question, because Governments are extremely squeezable on such matters. They always go in the direction of the least resistance, and when they find that a considerable section of their own followers are as determined as their opponents to obtain some measure of justice for agriculture, depend upon it we shall find then that our Constitution, which has lasted already a thousand years, will last a couple of years longer without any more tinkering, while our rulers devote themselves to the serious business of the country, which I take at this moment to be the concerting of measures for the relief of the agricultural interest. (Cheers.)

The Scheme.

And now, having traced the causes of the great depression under which we are suffering, I propose to indicate to you briefly the lines on which I think we may organise and combine so as to place ourselves in a position at least of self-defence. What I propose is, that agriculturists all over England should join in one great union on the basis of their common interests, and that membership shall be open to all persons who are interested in agriculture. The great principle on which I base that proposal has not been seriously attacked by any responsible person or any responsible paper—I mean the principle that the interests of those three classes are identically the same ; because what is the interest that each class has in the question now being debated ? We may be told that the landlord's interest is his rent, that the tenant's interest is his profits, and that the labourer's interest is his wages. All that is perfectly true, but there is one fund only out of which all three or any of them can possibly come, and that is the gains that arise from the cultivation of the soil. (Cheers.)

At this moment ʳthere is no question of a divided interest, or of what share each class shall take in the dividing of the profits. The profits have saved us all trouble in that respect by vanishing altogether. (Laughter.) The question for all three is this,—How are we to restore to the land those gains, out of which alone either rent, profits, or wages can be paid ? And if that be so, we ought to stand shoulder to shoulder in this matter. Other interests, some of them conflicting with ours, and all of them different, are organised, irrespective of us or against us, and we shall never get that bare measure of justice to which we are entitled in carrying on our industry unless we, too, unite on a common basis. (Cheers.)

Difficulties.

Of course, various details of the scheme have been criticised, and Lord Fitz-hardinge is well within his right in pointing out to you that, with regard to details, in a great movement like this, people will differ, and honestly differ. But I would point out this respectfully to those who differ with me on questions of detail. It appears to be admitted, as a matter of principle, that our interests are the same, and that it is necessary that we should be united. Difficulties there are, and nobody knows it better than I do; but would it not be a more useful exercise of ingenuity if people would set to work to suggest some way of getting over those which obviously exist, instead of showing their shrewdness by creating or imagining others ? (Cheers.)

If you and I are to go into this scheme with an honest desire to make it workable, let us look at obstacles from rather a different point of view, not trying to raise as many points as possible on which disunion might arise or difficulties be met with, but making honest attempts, which no one will welcome more heartily than I shall myself, to suggest the means by which they may be overcome ; and I say that because I am perfectly convinced that the difficulties are mere matters of detail, while the principle itself is unassailable ; that the thing can be done, that it will be done, that great results will flow from it, and that even these difficulties of detail are more formidable in appearance than in reality, and that as we face them—and we as Englishmen have faced difficulties before—we shall find them vanish before our united efforts.

Labourer's Point of View.

For instance, with regard to the scale of subscriptions, that is a detail which I quite admit may be open to criticism. You will remember that the scheme which I have placed before the country is only a draft scheme. I undertake to defend the principles of it. I have never undertaken to defend all its details. On the contrary, I have said that I would welcome suggestions from any quarter which may make the scheme more just to all classes, more simple, and more easily workable ; but upon this great principle I do ask you to take your stand with me, namely, first of all, as to the three classes engaged in this common industry that their interests are one and the same. They are, as it were, three partners engaged in the cultivation of the soil, each entitled to share the profits and losses of the business. The labourers say to me, and they are quite entitled to say it, "The last time that agriculture was prosperous, when corn was making a good price and things were high, we did not get that rise in our wages to which we think we were entitled." There is much truth in that contention. I will not go into the reasons. I simply state

"The NATIONAL AGRICULTURAL UNION CABLE"

A WEEKLY NEWSPAPER,

For Landowners, Farmers, Labourers, and all interested in the Prosperity of Agriculture.

Edited by the EARL of WINCHILSEA.

SUBSCRIPTION FORM

Which should be filled up and returned to Lord Winchilsea at the

Offices of "The National Agricultural Union Cable,"

30, FLEET STREET,

LONDON, E.C.

I shall be glad to become a Subscriber to "**The National Agricultural Union Cable.**"

Annual Subscription (Post Free), **6s. 6d.**

Name _____

Address _____

Any offers of help in making the Paper known will be gladly received. The first number will be published shortly.

it as an historical fact. And, therefore, when the labourers are asked to join with us in this Union, they say, naturally, "Shall we this time get our fair share of the profits if we assist you to make your business more profitable ?" Now, of course, in speaking upon this question, as I did at length at Ipswich, what took me something like an hour to explain is reported in the daily papers in the short space of half a column. It is inevitable that in a report of that kind naked statements should appear without the qualifications and explanations which I was able to give at the moment. I have, therefore, thought it respectful to those who may only have read such reports and been misled by them, to have the speeches which I delivered at York, at Ipswich, and at Plymouth, printed, and if you will do me the honour to read those three speeches *in extenso* as I delivered them, I believe that you will see that the propositions laid down are capable of being simply and easily defended. (Cheers.) We have brought down with us copies of those speeches, and any gentleman who is kind enough to take one will do me a service if he will read it, because then when he returns home he will be able to explain the project more fully to his neighbours than perhaps they now understand it.

Labourers' Subscriptions.

One gentleman made out in some calculations which he made that the scale of subscriptions would work out in this way : that the labourers, although their individual subscriptions were small, would in the aggregate pay the greatest share of all the three classes. Well, that might be the case in some villages where there is a large labouring population, but exactly the contrary would take place in the grass counties, where the labourers are few and landlords and tenants are relatively many.

Our Own Paper.

Besides, I would point out to those who may possibly take that view, that a proposal which I have made in connection with this Union, and which has generally recommended itself to those to whom I have explained it, does away with the inequality, if, indeed, it exists. What I propose to do is this : It would not be possible, of course, for me or for any one constantly to go about the country making speeches, even at important gatherings such as this, to explain the progress of the scheme. What will be absolutely necessary is this, that before it goes much further we should have an organ, a paper of our own, and that paper I propose very shortly to publish, and to edit myself. (Cheers.) I am quite certain that if you desire, as I do, to see agriculture, not the worst, but the best organised industry in this country, and if you consider that our organisation will stretch from the Land's End to Northumberland, and from Kent right up into Lancashire, then you will see how absolutely essential it is that every stage in that movement—all the proceedings of the Central Council and its resolutions, all the business of the various branches, all the great questions we shall specially debate at our meetings, and the progress we make with them—shall be placed before all members of the Union, week by week or month by month, in a paper sent to them from head-quarters. (Cheers.)

In the case of labouring men, who pay a penny a month to the Union, what we want is not so much their money as their help, their presence, and their support, and what I shall ask the Union to do is to send to every labourer who is a member of the Union a monthly copy of that paper in return for his penny subscription. And when I tell you that the paper will contain a good cartoon in every weekly number, and that we should reproduce the four weekly pictures in the monthly number, I am sure you will think that the labourer, at any rate, will then feel that he is quits with us beforehand. It is like putting your penny into the slot, and getting the sweetmeat out directly. He will then feel that whatever else we are able to do for him will be all to the good, because he will already have obtained his pennyworth from the Union to which he belongs. I am not fond of prophesying, but this I do say, there have been many movements in this country which have taken advantage of the press, but none, so far as I know, which has absolutely incorporated the press within itself. And knowing, as I do, something of the great power of the fourth estate of the realm, I think that I have done a very good bit of business when I have enlisted it thus on our behalf.

The "Missing Word" of Journalism.

And let me say this, in order that I may not wound the susceptibilities of any who may be responsible for or interested in agricultural papers at the present moment, that the great attention agriculture is now receiving owing to this movement, which has aroused the attention of the whole country from end to end, cannot fail to increase the circulation of any agricultural journal already in the field which records the progress of it. (Cheers.) I fear there is a little susceptibility in some quarters, because the moment that I announced that I was going to call the paper *The National Agricultural Union Gazette*, I had a letter from a paper which, I find, has a somewhat similar name, asking that I would drop the word " Gazette," or substitute another one for it. Well, in order to be obliging I immediately dropped the word " Gazette," and I intend to substitute for it a word which is entirely new, I believe, in the annals of journalism, and is not possessed by any other paper, not only in England, but throughout the world. It is a word which will at once indicate the strength of the threefold bond which unites us together, the freshness of our news, and the admirable, efficient, and lightning-like rapidity of our communication with our members from one end of England to the other. I leave you to guess what that word is. For the present it must remain the "missing word" of journalism. (A voice : Telephone.) No, Sir, it is not "Telephone " or "Telegraph." (Laughter.) My honourable friend is what you may call "rather warm," but he has not got the right word. (Laughter.)

Programme.

A great deal has been said about the programme of this Union when it is started, whom it is going to benefit, what it is going to be, what I ought to have put on it, and what I ought not to have put on it. One gentleman, speaking at the Central Chamber of Agriculture, said one of the truest things I have heard said about our programme when he remarked, "If you had no programme at all, we should all unanimously support it." (Hear, hear.) Well, a gentleman says "Hear, hear." Yes, that of course, may be so ; but still I think that unanimity in supporting nothing is not exactly the unanimity which we desire to establish. (Cheers and laughter.) The programme of the Union will be entirely in the hands of the Union itself, because from the moment that you adopt it, although the idea may come from me, it is your own Union, and no longer mine. All I venture to do, in the first place, is to place upon the programme measures in support of which I believe the agricultural interest is absolutely united. I take them from the unanimous resolutions of the Agricultural Conference, and as they are neither without interest nor without importance, I will tell you what they are.

"Union " not a "Programme."

But I do not, nor could anyone, confine the Union to that programme We must have a simple programme to start with, on which we are all unanimous, and having got your voting machinery and your means of holding meetings and passing resolutions, it will then be for the Union itself to place any article upon its programme that it desires. I am sure that you will be more obliged to me if I present you with a Union which has not got its hands, as it were, tied behind its back in every direction, and leave you free to form your own programme, with the exceptions which I have named, than if I were to put forward a cut-and-dried programme, which some of you, at any rate, would probably not agree with. If I were going to start an agricultural sect, pledged to follow me personally, it would be perfectly natural that I should lay down a fixed programme, and say, "Those who like it will follow me." But the central idea which I place before you is not a programme, but union ; the fact that the agricultural interest is disorganised, and ought to unite for common objects. (Cheers.) I appeal to no sect to follow me. I aspire to be no leader in any such sense. I place the idea of union before you ; I show you a path which we can tread with unanimity ; and I ask you carefully to consider, and then to place upon the programme of your Union afterwards, any other matters upon which you find agriculturists are agreed.

Local Burdens.

You will find, then, upon the programme of the Union the three resolutions to which I have referred ; and first, one in favour of the reduction of unfair burdens upon land. That is a subject upon which the Conference was unanimous, and if you will do me the honour, so that I may not detain you at greater length on that question, to read the speech which I delivered at York on the 5th of January, you will see that I there proved that the land tax, the poor rate, the education rate, and possibly other rates, ought not to be placed solely upon the land at all, that they were once national burdens and ought to be made so again ; and I pointed out that it would be a perfectly simple matter to combine local economy with efficiency, by making Imperial contributions to the extent which ought to defray those expenses from the Imperial Exchequer, leaving us if we could not so defray them to find the balance by a local rate. (A Voice: "That is the sort of thing we want.") Very well, then, let us all join together and get it. (Cheers.) People say to me, "Local burdens are a very small matter. Yes, but they are not so small a matter when you and I see the collector coming, and have, at a very inconvenient moment perhaps, to sign a cheque for £25 or £50 or whatever it may be. I say that they are not at all an unimportant matter. But that is not the only thing we are going to do. Let us do that first, and then, when the Union has once "tasted blood," it will soon go ahead and do other things.

Co-operation and Mr. Yerburgh.

There is another most important object in the forefront of our programme, to which I ask the particular attention of any labouring men who are here. I mean such co-operation between consumers and producers as shall save the unfair and often fraudulent profit of the middleman. I have been told that this question has not engaged a sufficient amount of my attention ; but, when you remember what the work of simply organising a great Union like this all over the kingdom is, and when you remember that from circumstances which I could not prevent a great portion of that work, notwithstanding the invaluable help that I have received from Mr. Rew, the Secretary of the Central Chamber of Agriculture, who is here (cheers), and also from my own secretary who sits beside me, has fallen upon myself, I am sure you will see that a difficult and complicated question like co-operation in all its details, as it is a matter of business and must be so dealt with, was one which could not hitherto have occupied a very large share of my own personal attention. But, from the very first moment that this movement was started, I had the cordial help and sympathy of two gentlemen, one of whom, Mr. Elwes, I am very glad to see on the platform here, and the other, Mr. Yerburgh, the member for Chester, has devoted himself in the meantime to this question of co-operation. He wrote a long and important article upon it, which I wish everybody would read, in the *Morning Post* of yesterday (8th February), giving an account of the system which prevails at the present moment in a neighbouring country, France ; and showing the extraordinary work that there is there being done, almost on the very lines of the proposed National Agricultural Union, by a combination between all the three classes connected with the land.

Land Banks.

They have what they call "land banks," and here is a point which I wish the labourers particularly to attend to. All the legislation which has at present been proposed for acquiring allotments and small holdings has been to a great extent a dead letter up to the present time, because it is not clear out of whose pockets the money is to come to enable the tenant to stock the small holdings. That is exactly the work that is taken up by these land banks in France. The report that Mr. Yerburgh quotes says, "They are still in their infancy, for they only have 400,000 members." A pretty healthy infant, I think, all the same. What they do is that on their mutual credit, on the credit of landlord, tenant, and labourer, over a large area, they provide money for their members on good security. Now, I say that there you would have an enormous engine for enabling hard working men who really desire to get hold of a small holding and stock it, to get a start in the world which they could not otherwise have, and without which almost all the Acts that can be passed with that object will be either waste paper, or will be carried out at the risk of the community at large.

This question is in its infancy, but it is one which the Union is pledged to take up from the first ; and I can assure you that I see in it the true way to make practicable many of those proposals for increasing the prosperity of the working classes which we have had such difficulty hitherto in carrying out.

Improved Compensation to Tenants.

With regard to other questions, I am told that we do not put a sufficient number of them on our programme. That is because we want a simple programme, first of all, which anybody can understand. But there are other questions of great importance. We could do much, for instance, to secure an improvement in the Acts providing compensation to tenants for improvements executed by them upon their holdings. (Cheers.) I admit that the Acts at present in force are defective, and I think that the common sense of all parties is in favour of more efficient legislation. But so long as we have these questions bandied about from one political party to another, candidates will bring them forward at election times and dangle them before you, but directly the election is over, and they have got in, they will throw them aside, and you will hear nothing about them till the next time your votes are required. (Cheers.)

Cheap Transfer of Land.

There are other matters which everybody would unite in desiring, and which this Union can be instrumental in obtaining. One is the cheapening of the transfer of land. Nothing prevents land from changing hands so much as the great expense and difficulty which attend the buying and selling of it. There are countries in which land is bought and sold as easily as a watch. I do not say that it could be the case in a country like our own, where there are very complicated and difficult rights, but I do say that the present expenses are monstrous, and that some means might and ought to be found for cheapening the transfer of land from one hand to another. (Cheers.)

Benevolent Fund.

Then, again, in a great Union of this kind, where you will have many poor members and many rich ones, why should you not do what you have never been able to do in any labourers' union yet : why should you not have a large Benevolent Fund? There are cases with which we all are personally acquainted, in which men who have made their payments, for instance, to a good friendly society for years, through stress of circumstances, owing to an illness, or an accident, are prevented from maintaining those payments. Everybody would wish that there should be a fund out of which those deserving persons could be enabled to tide over their difficulties.

Village Nurses.

The Union could do another thing which, in my own part of England at any rate, would bring more happiness into villages than almost any other expedient which could be devised. It is a question in which I hope shortly to interest the ladies of England in connection with this Union—and I am delighted to see so many ladies here present—to provide village nurses. (Cheers.) In many parts of England—I do not know how it may be here— we notice two things. First of all, the labourers do not like being sent to hospitals far away from their own villages ; and secondly, you very often find that a labourer, simply for want of knowing how unwell he really is, will go on working when really he is far too ill, and when a few days in bed, a few precautions taken in time, would have saved his health, and perhaps his life. These are not sensational matters ; they would not go down on political platforms ; but I do say, that if we could have a nurse in each of our villages to look after our working men and their families, we should have done an immense deal to remove the difficulties that now beset our labourers in time of illness. (Cheers.) Labouring men, in the exercise of their just and right independence, are enabled to hold their own in the world fairly enough, as long as they get good wages and permanent employment, until sickness comes upon them, but it is very difficult—and in many cases where there is a large family it is quite impossible—to make any provision during health for a sickness, which may come perhaps upon four or five members of the family at once. Where that is the case, then we may do much by providing not only a Benevolent Fund to which, I am sure, the richer members of a Union like this would be only too glad to subscribe, but such nursing too as will enable labourers and their families to be well taken care of and looked after during sickness, in their own villages and in their own homes. (Cheers.)

I fear I have detained you at great length upon these questions ; there is only one more with which I should like for one moment to deal, and that is the relations which may subsist between the National Agricultural Union and existing organisations.

Existing Organisations.

These have done excellent work, but they have, generally speaking, throughout the country admitted that their present basis and constitution, ever since the admission of labourers to the franchise, has been too narrow, and quite inadequate to deal with the questions that now arise, or to make existing bodies in any sense representative of the agricultural interest. Every Chamber of Agriculture, for instance, so far as I know, which has not accepted the scheme pure and simple, has passed a resolution in favour of widening and popularising its basis. I had a meeting with the Central Chamber, which, as you know, represents many existing institutions in this country, though not all of them ; and what I said was this : " I quite agree as to widening and popularising, but what does it mean, exactly? Does it mean my scheme, or have you one of your own ? Because, if you mean my scheme for widening and popularising, it will be very much better if you will say so, and then get to work to see how it can be done." That statement, I think, very much cleared the air, the Central Chamber of Agriculture accepted the principle, and appointed a committee to confer with me as to carrying the details of my scheme into effect. The proceedings of that committee, of course, are confidential until their report is presented, but it is a matter of public importance, and no breach of confidence on my part, that it should be known that we are working together in perfect harmony, and I believe shall arrive shortly at a result mutually satisfactory to us all. (Cheers.) My object is, I need not say, to unite all agriculturists and all existing associations that have done good work ; to unite and not to divide ; to bring them all into line ; so that the new organisation may in future combine within itself everything that is good, everything that is effective in the old organisations, and a great deal that is new to their character and constitution. (Cheers.)

I desire now very briefly, in leaving this question in your hands, to sum up what I have said and what I conceive to be the present position.

A Summary.

I have pointed out that the gravity of this crisis, however it may affect individuals, is of a national character, and cannot be seriously denied. I have shown that all agriculturists are interested in staying the progress of it if they can ; that all are in danger of seeing their gains sink to a vanishing point, and that with them will disappear the only fund out of which rent, profits, or wages can be paid. I have conceded that to foreign competition— some of it fair which we cannot do much to mitigate, some of it unfair which we may do much to prevent—is partly due the present state of agriculture. But I have pointed out—and I have given you such examples as I think suffice to prove it—that it is also to the disorganised state of your great industry that many of the chief evils from which you are suffering are traceable.

I have, therefore, on the principle that their interests are one and the same, advocated the formation of a Union of all three classes connected with the land ; and described to you how that Union may be effected. Into the details of its working I have not thought it necessary to enter to-day, but any gentleman who desires to know what they are can have copies of the draft scheme, in which he will see the different centres that we take, and the exact and, I hope, simple machinery by which we hope to bring the Union home to every village in this country. I have also indicated what, in my judgment, are the items which should, and those which should not, at first at any rate, form a part of the programme. It is now for you, gentlemen, to weigh the facts, and to ask yourselves whether the time has not come for making a decisive, perhaps it may be a final, effort to avert ruin from the great industry by which we live. I am quite certain that if all three classes, instead of turning their backs upon each other, will turn round and face each other like men—(loud cheers)—we shall find that many of our differences exist not in reality, but only in the fact that we have been too long estranged from each other.

We must Succeed.

We may or we may not succeed in lifting agriculture out of the plight into which it has fallen ; but in one thing we must succeed, and that is sufficient reward, I think, for any one who will attempt it: we must succeed in introducing a better spirit into our rural life, and in doing away with much of the bitterness which now separates one class from another. We do well to recollect that in this country matters have now reached a point at which class hatred seems to be very near to us, and all the old links that bound us together seem ready to yield to the slightest strain; and when you remember further that that is, and has always been found in history to be, the very point at which a nation begins to go back and to decay,—then if you put your shoulders to this work, you may or may not save the industry to which you belong, but you will feel that, at any rate, at a time of great difficulty and of grave peril you have done your duty to yourselves, to your neighbours, and to your country. (Loud cheers.)

www.ingramcontent.com/pod-product-compliance
Lightning Source LLC
Chambersburg PA
CBHW031441270326
41930CB00007B/816